The

Vegetarian Philosophy of India

The
Vegetarian
Philosophy
of India

Hindu,
Buddhist
& Jain
Sacred Teachings

by Holly Roberts

Anjeli Press

THE

VEGETARIAN
PHILOSOPHY
OF INDIA

HINDU,
BUDDHIST
& JAIN
SACRED TEACHINGS

WRITTEN AND ILLUSTRATED
BY HOLLY ROBERTS, D.O., PH.D.

Published by
Anjeli Press
www.Anjelipress.com

ISBN 0-9754844-2-7

Printed in the United States of America
by Lightning Source
Distributed by Ingram Distributors

Dedicated to

Dr. Nirmala Sanakkayala

through whom I learned

the peace and kindness

of one who lives the Hindu Faith

The Vegetarian Philosophy of India

Throughout all ages
and amongst all peoples
teachings of concern, compassion and kindness
have been fostered.

Yet it has been solely upon the subcontinent of India
that teachings of compassion and kindness
toward all forms of beings
have thrived.

It is because of these teachings
that billions of people upon the subcontinent of India
have chosen to live their entire lives
without taking the life of any other being.

And it has been through such teachings,
that India's people have learned that the blessings of
compassion and kindness must be shared with all creatures.
Indeed, with all creation.

In seeking to understand where such values originated,
one must search the ancient scriptural passages
of India's three great vegetarian faiths,
Hinduism, Buddhism and Jainism, for answers.

This book represents the result of such a search.

Its pages contain the wisdom of ancient scriptural passages
of Hindu, Buddhist and Jain faiths
that have formed the foundation of the spiritually profound
Vegetarian Philosophy of India.

Holly Roberts

Please note that, in some cases, different sources used different transliterations of the same Sanskrit term.

THE VEGETARIAN PHILOSOPHY OF INDIA

Table of Contents

PART II
SACRED TEACHINGS LEADING TO THE VEGETARIAN PHILOSOPHY OF INDIA

PART III
CONCLUSION

PART IV
BACK MATTER

LISTS & MAPS

INTRODUCTION

The Lord of Love shines in the hearts of all. Seeing Him in all creatures, the wise forget themselves in the service of all.
Mundaka Upanishad[1]

Have you ever wondered why India has been the sole nation upon earth where billions of people have chosen to live their entire lives as vegetarians? I, too, have wondered why. When questioned about their vegetarian lifestyles, people of Indian heritage simply and quietly state that being vegetarian is part of whom they are. It is the essence of their faith. The philosophy of vegetarianism is as natural to these individuals as the philosophy of not harming and not killing humans is to those of other faiths. Their choice to live as vegetarians has given them such inner peace that they feel no need to question the origin of their beliefs.

One seeking to understand exactly why and how such values arose on the subcontinent of India must search the sacred teachings of India's oldest religion, Hinduism, for answers. For it is within the millennia old teachings of this most ancient religion, Hinduism, that the ethical and spiritual values of the people of India took form.

Delving into the sacred wisdom of the Hindu faith is a fascinating, yet not a simple, endeavor. That is because the ancient teachings of Hinduism are both voluminous and profound. The Hindu faith emerged over 10,000 years ago and evolved gradually. Hinduism contains the most ancient, and largest, body of literature ever recorded by humankind. Just attempting a study of the *Vedas* transports one into a world of deeply philosophical concepts, for the *Vedas* contain teachings that evolved over millenia from the accumulated wisdom of numerous ancient Indian sages. Yet such a course of study is worth it.

Within the Hindu faith, God is perceived as being present in everyone and everything. Because God is perceived as being present in all creation, God is also seen as being capable of manifesting in infinite numbers of forms. Keeping this concept in mind, a Hindu respects not only his or her perception of God, but also other's perception of God. Hindus believe that God is so great that God can, and does, present to all differently.

Accordingly, any form through which God has presented to another, no matter how different that is from the form through which God has presented to oneself, is recognized and respected. That has been why, over the centuries, Hinduism has grown into a faith that has incorporated an expansive canon of sacred literature, a large pantheon of gods, and a variety of diverse philosophies.

Another reason why Hinduism is fascinating is because over the centuries Hindus, knowingly or unknowingly, have embraced concepts of the Buddhist and Jain faiths. Actually, the latter two faiths took many of their beliefs from Hinduism. Hence, to study effectively the origin and evolution of vegetarian values within India, one must consider the impact Hindu, Buddhist and Jain faiths have had upon one another.

In initiating a study of Hinduism, one must search back to the era of 8,000 BCE. That is when the ancient people of India first began to develop their philosophical and metaphysical belief systems. Their teachings emerged and evolved amongst small communities of people living along the banks of the Sindhu (Indus) and Saraswati Rivers in northwest India. They also emerged within villages in the mountainous regions of northern India, the Punjab.

The former evolved into what would later become known as the "Indus Valley Civilization" and the latter, into the "Aryan Civilization." Is is important to note that the Aryans were individuals of Indian origin—native to the mountainous lands of northern India. They were not, as had been hypothesized by some, individuals of European extraction.

When the Indus Valley civilization and the Aryan civilization merged, they assimilated their views of God, of creation, and of humankind's place within eternity. Because these people accepted that no one set of sacred teachings held all answers, they valued and absorbed one another's wisdom. In so doing, they reached higher levels of understanding of profound truths than that attainable solely through the study of one faith.

The soul of religions is one, but encased in a multitude of forms.
Mahatma Gandhi[2]

Part I

Background

The Hindu Faith

PART I

BACKGROUND

THE HINDU FAITH

ORIGINS OF THE HINDU FAITH

Millennia back, in the far northwestern reaches of the Indian subcontinent, the seeds of philosophical wisdom that would someday blossom into the religion known as Hinduism had begun to germinate. This wisdom began to take root amongst people living in humble communities in northwestern India scattered along riverbanks and nestled away in India's lofty, northern mountain peaks.[1]

The people of these ancient communities were both philosophical and spiritual. Archeological evidence indicates that they were also deeply analytical and observant. They observed and analyzed the patterns of the solar system, as well as the fate of humankind. It was based upon these observations, that they built their faith.

These people recognized that a grand, natural order prevailed and that this order regulated all creation. They also recognized that through understanding of this order, one might gain insight into the infinitely perpetual cycling of the cosmos. These people felt humbled when they recognized the meager role humankind held within this grand order. It was based upon such humility and such understanding—understanding that accumulated over millennia—that the people of ancient India founded their faith.

The land in which these people lived was known as the Sapta Sindhu, the "Region of Seven Rivers." They lived in small sophisticated communities along the banks of the Indus (Sindhu) River and the Saraswati River. Their communities studded these riverbanks all the way from small tributaries high in the Himalayan Mountains to those adjacent to the large river basins feeding into the Arabian Sea. Possibly five hundred such communities existed.

Their civilization has been referred to as the Indus (Sindhu) Valley civilization, or the civilization of the Indus River. Recently, however, as historians have discovered there were actually two rivers in this region—the Indus River and the Saraswati River—their civilization has been referred to as the Saraswati-Sindhu Valley civilization.

Over time, members of these communities migrated eastward. Some settled along the Ganges River, while others migrated southward to the plains near present day Chennai (formerly Madras).

In discussing the philosophy of Hinduism, one must clarify some important misconceptions concerning its origins. The major misconception has been a hypothesis that individuals referred to as invading Aryans imported much of India's wisdom from lands north and northwest of India, into the Indian subcontinent.

This misconception had been based upon well-meaning, yet unfounded, Eurocentric perspectives. In creating such hypotheses, various historians assigned credit for the Hindu *Vedas* (the foundational scriptures of Hinduism) to an elusive group of invaders from either Central Asia or North-central Europe. They termed these individuals "Aryans."

The legend of such an invasion became entrenched within both Western and Indian historical texts. Yet no such foreign invasion has ever been substantiated either within the history of India or the history of any theoretical invading nation. To the contrary, present-day linguistic, literary, archaeological, geologic, and astronomic evidence has shown unequivocally that India's spiritually advanced teachings were derived from people of Indian heritage.

These spiritually advanced individuals were people native to the mountains of northern India and had lived for centuries in present-day Punjab. It was from such people that the wisdom of the Hindu *Vedas* was born. Merging their wisdom with the spiritual and philosophical insight of the people of the Indus-Saraswati Valley, they ushered in the philosophical era known as the Vedic Period of India's history.

For centuries, historians believed that because the wise individuals who wrote the *Vedas* spoke of an unknown river, the Saraswati, these individuals had come from distant lands. But now it is recognized that during the Vedic period, possibly as far back as the twelfth century BCE, both the Indus River and the Saraswati River flowed in northwestern India. Flowing east of and parallel to the Indus River, the Saraswati River completely dried up thousands of years ago, leaving behind what probably has become the Great Indian Desert in present day Rajasthan. Scientists believe that the river dried up due to changes in climatic conditions resulting, predominantly, from shifting tectonic plates.

Hence, scholars now recognize that the authors of the *Vedas* were of Indian heritage.

The Saraswati River is mentioned as far back as the oldest of the *Vedas*, the *Ṛg Veda*.

> *Of the rivers, the Saraswati alone knows (this)—the sacred stream*
> *that flows from the mountains into the sea.*
>
> *Ṛg Veda*[2]

The ancient people who reduced the *Vedas* to writing evolved their wisdom over centuries.[3] The style in which they wrote reveals that they were not invaders in search of conquest. It also reveals that they were not people of distant lands longing to return to a homeland outside of India. Rather, their passages reveal that they were people who loved the lands, the culture, and the beliefs of India. Essentially, it was people native to the lands of India who composed the Hindu *Vedas*.

THE INDUS VALLEY CIVILIZATION

During the prehistoric Great Ice Age, thick sheets of ice covered Northern India. By the Second Interglacial Period, 400,000 to 200,000 BCE, human life was first able to sustain itself upon the Indian subcontinent. Through a series of climatic changes and a shifting in tectonic plates, the climate of Northwestern India gradually became more temperate. Vast forests began to proliferate and villages began to thrive along low-lying riverbanks.

The people of northwestern India developed a highly advanced culture known as the Harappa and Mohenjo-daro culture. Their lives were enriched by beautiful writings and profound astronomic observations. Present-day astronomers have determined that the events they described within their writings could have occurred no later than approximately 5,000 BCE, and these would have been visible only in the northern mountains of India. Correlation of the following passage of the *Ṛg Veda* to astronomic events indicates that it was composed thousands of years ago.

> *Brhaspati, or the Planet Jupiter, was first discovered when con-*
> *fronting or nearly occulting the star Tisya.*
>
> *Taittiriya Brahamana*[4]

Astronomic correlations place the writing of other passages of the *Vedas*, the *Vrsakapi Hymn* (x. 86), at approximately 16,000 BCE and of the *Marriage Hymn* (x.85, 13) at approximately 15,000 BCE.[5] Through such findings, scholars believe that various passages of the *Ṛg Veda* (the earliest *Veda*) were probably composed sometime between 25,000 to 7,500 BCE.

Linguistic studies of the *Vedas* point to the highly advanced nature of India's ancient civilization. Because the language of the *Vedas* is so advanced, linguists feel that their literary acumen must have been evolving over thousands of years even before their words were reduced to writing.

Locations and Characteristics of Indus Valley Civilizations

Artifacts from the Harappa and Mohenjo-daro cultures, such as agricultural tools, have been found all the way from the low-lying riverbanks near the Arabian Sea to the mountains of Kashmir and Punjab. They have also been found in southern India, near present day Chennai (formerly Madras). During ancient times, however, a vast, shallow sea covered much of central India. This sea submerged the lands adjacent to the Ganges River.[6] People of the Indus Valley civilizations, nevertheless, still managed to migrate to central India south of the Ganges Valley, and to east India near present day Assam, Bihar and Orissa.[7]

By 1,600 BCE, inhabitants of the Indus Valley civilization and peoples of the Mesopotamian city of Sumeria, engaged in significant levels of communication and interaction with one another. Hence, it is not surprising that beliefs of the Indus Valley people were similar to those of Middle Eastern and Mediterranean civilizations. Both developed similar fertility rites and worship of a Mother Goddess. In both, the maternal figure was sometimes represented as a cow.[8]

After many centuries, the Indus Valley civilization seemed to dwindle. It is believed that as the Saraswati River dried up, the lands were no longer capable of sustaining the population. Hence, the people migrated. According to radiocarbon dating, by 2,000 to 1,700 BCE, the Indus Valley civilization had decreased in size significantly. It is possible, however, that a series of natural catastrophes, rather than just one, led to the demise of this great civilization.[9]

Attitudes toward Animals within Indus Valley Communities

These ancient times witnessed the birth of many diverse attitudes towards animals. Artifacts reveal that animals were thought of as beasts of burden, as food, as family pets, and as respected beings.[10] Passages of the *Ṛg Veda* indicate that the cow was domesticated and considered of great significance. It was referred to as a source of milk and butter for nutrition, of clarified butter (ghee) for kindling sacrificial flames, and of dried dung for fuel and fertilizer. Some historians believe that the cow was considered sacred because of all the benefits it added to society.[11]

Archaeological ruins from these ancient communities contain bones of animals. Yet historians cannot determine the relationship of the humans of that civilization to the animals. Terra cotta seals, used as identification stamps, indicate that various animals were tamed for domestic purposes. They also reveal that some animals were considered sacred.[12] Several terra cotta seals depict bulls adorned with ornaments, possibly indicating that bulls were used during times of sacred worship.[13] (Note)[14]

Although some findings indicate that a percentage of people within the Indus Valley civilization were carnivorous, other findings indicate that some were not. Some people held great reverence for animals, particularly domesticated ones. They bonded tremendously with dogs.[15] In some villages, dogs were buried with their owners, while in others, people dedicated specific burial sites for dogs and wolves.[16]

Spiritual Attitudes within Indus Valley Communities

Terra cotta seals of contemplative, meditative sages have been uncovered from various Indus Valley ruins. One seal depicts a meditating yogi surrounded by animals. Such seals indicate that these people engaged in advanced spiritual practices such as meditation. With recent evidence indicating that "Aryans" were individuals of Indian origin, rather than of European origin, historians recognize that practices of contemplation and meditation originated on the subcontinent of India.[17]

The seal of the meditating sage surrounded by animals may be an early indication that a philosophy of communion with, and nonviolence towards, all beings may have been evolving within ancient Indian communities.[18] Additional artifacts indicate that a philosophy of asceticism was evolving as well. These artifacts, and the writings of the *Vedas*, indicate a diversity of attitudes existed within ancient India. Some individuals believed in animal sacrifice while others believed in nonviolent, ascetic and pacific practices.[19]

Lifestyles within Indus Valley Communities

The lifestyle within most early Indian communities seems to have been peaceful. People developed cities, created drainage systems, and worshiped a mother-goddess. In low-lying regions, people domesticated cattle, sheep, and goats. In mountainous regions, people created hilltop settlements, leveled terraces, cultivated forests, and created cattle stations for seasonal grazing. Some raised cattle (depicted in terra cotta figurines from 2300—1800 BCE) and others cultivated grain and millet.[20]

Those residing in eastern India in the hills of Assam were farmers. They used agricultural tools similar to those used in China and South-east Asia. Those of the rugged mountains of Kashmir based their culture upon hunting. And those of south-central India were shepherds, raising cattle, sheep, and goats.[21]

THE ARYAN CIVILIZATION

That part of India's history written by Europeans tells that in approximately 2,000 BCE, Indo-European invaders, termed "Aryans," invaded the Indus Valley. It tells that they came from lands of Northern Europe or lands adjacent to the Black and Caspian Seas. It also tells that they brought the *Vedas* with them into India.[22]

This history was based upon a misinterpretation of the reason the Indus Valley civilization began to dwindle, of linguistic relationships between Sanskrit and other Indo-European language, and of similarities between Iranian and Indian civilizations.[23] Some of these historians even theorize that these invading Aryans mixed with local Indians, and formed the ancient empire of the Hittites.

These historians thought that the term "Aryan" referred to people with ethnically lighter skin tone than the people of the Indus Valley. Recently, however, linguists have recognized that the term "Aryan" did not refer to racial characteristics. Rather, it referred to moral characteristics. In India's ancient writings, an Aryan was one of honorable and gentle character.

The only event during this phase of India's history that seems to correspond to any invasion may have been the period of dominance by the *Kshatriyas* of northern India.[24] Historians are not sure if the *Kshatriyas* originated from inside or outside India's borders.

ORIGIN AND SPREAD OF THE INDUS VALLEY CIVILIZATION

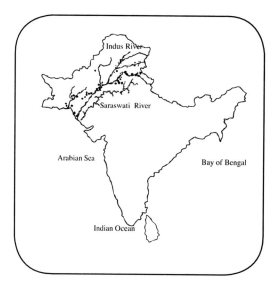

Sites of the original Indus Valley communities scattered along the Indus and Saraswati Riverbanks. The Saraswati River, prior to having dried up, flowed parallel to, and east of, the Indus River. (The course of the Saraswati River as depicted above is an approximation).

Sites throughout India where members of the Indus Valley civilization migrated and set up communities.

Adapted from Bridget Allchin and Raymond Allchin, *The Birth of Indian Civilization* (Baltimore, MD: Penguin Press, 1968), 176.[25]

SACRED WRITINGS OF THE HINDU FAITH

A foundational concept within Hinduism is that there are many roads to truth. Hinduism teaches one to respect and welcome the spiritual beliefs of all others, even those beliefs contrary to one's own. It teaches that God can manifest in an infinite number of ways. Hence, it is inevitable that various people perceive the Great Unknown differently. Because of Hinduism's acceptance and reverence for beliefs of others, it has thrived as a religion of colorful, fascinating diversity.

With acceptance and incorporation of beliefs of others, the Hindu faith grew to encompass a large and diverse body of sacred scriptures. These include the *Vedas*; the *Upanishads* (end of the *Vedas*); the *Puranas*; the epic stories of the *Ramayana*, the *Mahabharata*, the *Bhagavad Gita*; the philosophy of Vedanta; the *Laws of Manu*; the *Tirukkural*, and the *Yoga Sutras*.

Many of these writings evolved over generations, even centuries. While some writings are philosophically and spiritually similar, others are quite different. Followers of the Hindu faith accept and respect the philosophical perspectives of all.

A foundational concept within Hinduism is that God presents to all differently—in different forms, at different times, and with different messages. All of these presentations are respected. As this philosophy spread across India, the people of its lands embraced one another's sacred teachings. Their resultant belief system, Hinduism, became a rich tapestry of multicolored beliefs and traditions. It became a tapestry woven with threads of wisdom of diverse shades and hues.[26]

To one of Western heritage, Hinduism may appear as a baffling tangle of myths, with endless gods and goddesses worshipped in countless forms. But it is this rich complexity that has guided and unified the Indian people for thousands of years.[27]

What may appear to one unfamiliar with the Hindu faith as differences, are actually a tribute to Hinduism's all embracing philosophy. Hinduism's respect for the beliefs of others has helped those of Hindu faith to survive and co-exist in harmony with people of other faiths for over four thousand years.[28]

Within Hinduism, various theories of metaphysics co-exist. Its pantheon of deities contains two main categories of gods—gods of the *Vedas* and gods of the *Puranas*. Its philosophical teachings contain various perspectives towards incarnation, cosmology, reality, Yoga, and numerous other concepts. And its literature includes numerous holy sages, saints, cities, rivers, and sites for pilgrimages.

Yet in spite of this apparent diversity, certain principles are foundational within all aspects of the Hindu faith. These include a profound respect for God, compassion towards all people, appreciation of metaphysical principles, and concern for all creation. The following is an overview of those writings that constitute the sacred scriptures of Hinduism.

The Vedas

The *Vedas* are the foundational sacred writings of the Hindu faith. Their philosophical concepts are viewed as having been derived directly from Rishis, ancient seers, rather than merely through thoughts of humankind. Rishis are those individuals through whom God transmitted messages. As seers of truth, Rishis revealed the wisdom they obtained through the *Vedas* so as to share it with humankind.[29] The *Vedas* are considered divine revelations of truths from God, as transmitted through Rishis.

> *The Vedas are the eternal truths revealed by God to the great ancient*
> *Rishis of India. The Rishi did not write. He did not create it out of*
> *his own mind. He was the seer of thought that already existed.*[30]

Veda is a Sanskrit word. Its root *vid* means, "to know." The *Vedas* contain ancient hymns, commentaries, and wisdom. They contain sacred knowledge perceived as having been revealed to humankind from the beginning of time. They are considered eternal—without beginning or end. Some perceive them as emanating from the breath of God.[31] By the end of the third century BCE, the canon of Vedic literature was considered closed. After that, however, the *Vedas* became the philosophical foundation upon which much of the later Hindu thought has been founded.

There are four *Vedas*, each originating from a specific family tradition. These are the *Ṛg Veda, Sama Veda, Yajur Veda,* and *Atharva Veda.*[32] The earliest is the *Ṛg Veda.*

There are also four divisions of each *Veda*. Each division is perceived as corresponding to one of the four major stages in an individual's life. The *Vedas* were memorized and passed on as oral tradition from generation to generation. Initially, historians believed that the *Ṛg Veda* was composed 1500—1000 BCE. More recently, geological and astronomic evidence indicates that the *Vedas* were composed many thousands of years ago. Furthermore, scholars recognize that it had been transmitted orally millennia prior to that time.

The *Ṛg Veda*, Seventh *Mandala*, verse 2, *Sukta* 95 tells that the Saraswati River flowed from the Himalayan Mountains to the sea.[33] It is known, however, through archaeological and astrological evidence, that 7,500 years ago volcanic and seismic upheavals caused the Saraswati River to dry up. Such passages indicate that the *Ṛg Veda* had to have been composed, at least in oral form, prior to 5,000 BCE.

THE VEDAS AND THE EARLY INDIAN PHILOSOPHY TOWARD ANIMALS

The *Vedas* reveal that people of ancient India held great respect, and fear, for the forces of nature. They envisioned the forces of nature as God.[34] Their ancient practices of animal sacrifice were oftentimes done to appease the gods.[35] There is no evidence during Hinduism's earliest years, when the earliest Vedas were being formulated, that cows were inherently sacred. They were considered sacred only when they were sacrificed.

The *Vedas* contain information explaining the ancient beliefs and practices related to the rituals of animal sacrifice. These sacrifices often involved large numbers of animals—from elephants to insects.[36] The sacrifices were not viewed as acts of violence, but as acts of reverence. The horse sacrifice (*Ashvamedha*) was the most well known sacrifice.[37] The practice of animal sacrifice was not abnormal during these ancient eras, as it was practiced within various eastern cultures.[38]

Vedic writings, however, seem to indicate that although some people practiced sacrifice, others expressed an aversion to the taking of an animal's life. Some people definitely questioned the consumption of flesh.[39] Epitaphs from early Vedic ruins bear phrases that cows were "not to be killed." It is unclear, however, if such declarations were created for ethical reasons, pacific reasons, or merely for economic reasons.[40]

THE FOUR DIVISIONS OF EACH VEDA

There are four divisions within each of the four *Vedas*.[41] Modern day scholars often exclude those divisions that consist predominantly of chants and sacrificial prayers. Yet after one achieves full understanding of them, one can gain insight into exalted spiritual truths.[42]

THE FOUR DIVISIONS OF EACH OF THE FOUR VEDAS

Mantra Samhitas	(Hymns of Praise)
Brahmanas	(Guides to sacrificial rites)
Aranyakas	(Interpretations of rituals)
Upanishads	(Philosophy of the *Vedas*)

MANTRA SAMHITAS

Mantra Samhitas are hymns of Praise to God. They offer thanks for all that God has given one during one's lifetime and for peace in the hereafter.[43] They contain philosophical analyses of God, nature, and humankind. The *Samhitas* express the belief that a grand order pervades the universe, and that all creation is one unified entity within this order.

BRAHMANAS

The *Brahmanas* contain hymns used during sacrifices that were perceived to appease God. They also discuss sacrifices and sacrificial rites. Ancient Hindus believed that one attained purification through acts of charity and through acts of sacrifice. They believed that humans owed a debt to the gods—a debt repayable by feeding the gods.[44] Brahmins (priests) controlled the performance of sacrifices. Over time, original meanings of the *Brahmanas* were lost and only ritual aspects and sacrifices remained.[45]

ARANYAKAS

The *Aranyakas* are often termed the Forest Books. They contain interpretations of sacrificial rites. They reveal that various rites within the *Brahmanas* were symbols of those means used to assist one in meditation. Oftentimes, they are somewhat critical of ceremony and ritual, stating that these only create a veil between oneself and the ultimate truth. They stress one's retiring into one's own self, stating that all truth lies within the human soul.[46]

UPANISHADS

The *Upanishads* are the final portion of each *Veda*. They contain the philosophical teachings of Hinduism that have guided Indian thought for thousands of years. They include Hindu concepts of God, the soul, *karma*, rebirth, and nonviolence. *Upanishads* of the *Artharva Veda* are the earliest known Hindu writings that refer to the cow as being sacred. Its passages warn that one who kicks a cow will no longer cast a shadow upon the earth.[47]

The term *Upanishad* was derived from the term *upa* meaning near, *ni* for down, and *sad* for sit. That was because the wisdom of the *Upanishads* was transferred from generation to generation orally, and pupils would sit on the ground near the teacher to learn ancient sacred teachings.[48]

There are actually over two hundred *Upanishads*, but Indian scholars consider one hundred and eight *Upanishads* as the traditional ones. Each of the four *Vedas* contains its own set of *Upanishads*, with each focusing upon somewhat different philosophical concepts. The *Upanishads* contain a compendium of ancient Indian philosophical thought. They represent a scholarly work that grew in segments. Each *Upanishad* contains the teachings of deeply spiritual thinkers who were concerned about many of life's philosophical problems. Hence both their orientations, as well as their solutions, often vary. Those *Upanishads* that embody the highest values of sacred teachings are considered the principal *Upanishads*.

THE PRINCIPAL UPANISHADS

Isha (Isavasya) Upanishad
Kena (Keno) Upanishad
Katha (Katho) Upanishad
Prashna Upanishad
Mundaka Upanishad
Mandukya Upanishad
Taittiriya Upanishad
Aitareya Upanishad
Chandogya Upanishad
Brihadaranyaka Upanishad
Shvetashvatara Upanishad

THE PURANAS

The *Puranas* represent a compendium of ancient Hindu beliefs, philosophy, folklore, mythology and history. They include a plethora of rich teachings passed down in oral form from ancient Vedic times—between the twelfth and fourth centuries BCE. Their concepts were derived from diverse communities, rather than from just one particular group.

> *Hindu thought believes in the evolution of our knowledge of God. It accepts the obvious fact that humankind seeks its goal of God at various levels and in various directions, and feels sympathy with every stage in the search.*
>
> Radhakrishnan[49]

The *Puranas* consist of a large body of literature filled with concepts such as Hindu mythology, idol worship, love of God, superstition, festivals, ceremonies, philosophy, and ethics.[50] They also serve as an encyclopedic source of ancient Indian thought.

The *Puranas* contain theories of creation, analyses of genealogies, and the histories of India's ancient kings and kingdoms.[51] They are divided into two major categories. Each contains eighteen *Puranas* and all contain a wealth of information concerning Hindu doctrine and mythology.[52]

THE GREAT EPICS

The *Mahabharata*, the *Ramayana*, and the *Bhagavad Gita* are Hinduism's great literary epics. They were written after the *Vedas* during an era appropriately called the "Epic Period." Many of their principles are based upon the *Vedas*. The *Bhagavad Gita*, in particular, is founded upon philosophical principles of the *Upanishads*.

The wisdom and teachings of the epics are not considered to be divine revelations obtained directly from God, as are the *Vedas*. Rather, they are considered secondary sources of wisdom obtained from prophets, saints, sages, and Divine Incarnations.[53] They contain a wealth of wisdom and they have guided Hindu philosophical and spiritual thought for centuries.

The *Mahabharata* and the *Ramayana* are the two large epics. The *Bhagavad Gita* is actually derived from one chapter of the *Mahabharata*. Yet the *Bhagavad Gita* contains such profound philosophical wisdom that is considered an entity unto itself. Some scholars believe it may have been created at a date later than the rest of the *Mahabharata*.[54] Though not voluminous, the *Bhagavad Gita* is of tremendous spiritual value.

THE MAHABHARATA

The *Mahabharata* is a tale of epic proportions. It transports its readers into a series of soul-searching and heart wrenching family conflicts. Within the midst of these family conflicts, numerous heroic characters enter into, intertwine with, and depart from, the epic. The reader is drawn into the story, and feels the emotions and inner conflicts of each charatcer.

Inevitably, those family conflicts that remained unresolved within one generation, lead to tragic repercussions in the next. The result is an all encompassing war. In the war, all family members, friends, and even teachers must take sides. The setting for the *Mahabharata*'s final set of chapters is that of a brutal battlefield. The story is based upon a war that actually took place during the ninth century BCE in central India near the Ganges River.

Throughout the epic, one learns values such as justice, compassion, self-restraint, truthfulness, abstention from injury, moderation, non-attachment, asceticism, rejection of desire for wealth, and acceptance of one's destiny.[55] The finale of the *Mahabharata* takes place after the end of the devastating war. This was a time of tragedy—a time filled with deep remorse. Many relatives on both sides had been slaughtered. Within these passages, Hindu values of righteousness, peace, and nonviolence toward all beings are expressed. Although the conflict involves a terrible war, the moral teachings are profoundly spiritual.[56]

> *Abstention from injury, by act, thought, and word, in respect of all creatures . . . constitute behavior that is worthy of praise.*
> *Mahabharata*[57]

Recognizing the tragedy of violence, the *Mahabharata* teaches the virtue of peace:

> *Consider the lives of all the great kings who have ruled this world. Those who were really great are the peace-loving kings. I see that the policy of peace is the most desirable thing in the world.*
> *Mahabharata*[58]

The Ramayana

Though the events described in the *Ramayana* occurred very early in India's history, its passages were not reduced to writing until the sixth century BCE. It reached its final form during the first century CE.[59] The *Ramayana* has remained a source of spiritual and ethical inspiration for millennia.

Its three principal characters, Rama, Sita, and Hanuman, have molded the spiritual character of Hindus for centuries. Rama is the embodiment of truth and morality. He is the ideal son, husband, father, and king. Sita is a woman of purity, patience, and sacrifice. Hanuman, though a primate, embodies heroism, self-effacing sacrifice, and loyalty.[60]

THE BHAGAVAD GITA

The *Bhagavad Gita* is a work of profound metaphysical and spiritual depth. As a part of the *Mahabharata*, the *Bhagavad Gita's* philosophical teachings are based upon the challenges an individual, Arjuna, faces within this epic. Some believe it was written later than the main portion of the *Mahabharata*, and finally completed by 200-400 CE.

Through the backdrop of a war, its passages explain many of the foundational concepts of Hinduism, including the concept that God exists within all beings. The *Bhagavad Gita* explains that God is the inner essence of all in existence. Hence, all creation is a manifestation of God.[61]

The *Bhagavad Gita* is written as a dialogue between Krishna and his friend and disciple, Arjuna. Arjuna represents all human beings in their struggle to understand the meaning of life, and their own place within it. Krishna is an avatar, a divine incarnation, of the Hindu God Vishnu. He teaches Arjuna that God lives within all beings.

As the *Bhagavad Gita* unfolds, its characters are involved in a tragic war. Krishna, speaking as a manifestation of God, advises Arjuna that in spite of the suffering that war causes, it is sometimes necessary to fight. This is one of those times. Krishna explains that beyond life and death, there exists a higher principle of right and wrong.

The true war being fought in the *Bhagavad Gita* is the war that each individual must fight within oneself. It is the battle within one's own conscience to fulfill one's responsibilities and fully live out one's destiny. Krishna explains how one may attain purity of heart. By "renouncing all egoism, power, pride, lust, wrath, and property, freed from the idea of 'me and mine,' and attaining tranquility of heart, [one becomes] fit realizing his oneness with Brahman."[62]

Yoga Sutras

The *Yoga Sutras* consist of one hundred and ninety-five brief aphorisms of ancient wisdom. These were compiled and recorded by Patanjali. According to many scholars, they were formulated approximately 150 BCE. Some scholars, however, place their composition later. Yoga is that branch of Hindu literature and sacred teachings designed to lead one away from living solely in a lower state of consciousness. It teaches that through control of one's mind and one's body, one can attain realization of great truths.

Yoga is first mentioned in the *Vedas* in a passage of the *Katha Upanishad.* It is described as a chariot that possesses the reasoning ability to lead a cart. The passage explains that through control of the senses, one can master the body.[63] The *Bhagavad Gita* discusses the values of yoga, specifically of *karma* yoga (the yoga of self-control) and *bhakti* yoga (the yoga of devotion to one's god).

The *Yoga Sutras* describe philosophical-ethical branches of Yoga. These are virtues one must develop within oneself to attain higher levels of understanding. The first branch of Yoga involves cultivation of self-restraints. Among these, *ahimsa* is considered the first step. *Ahimsa*, as described within the *Yoga Sutras*, includes abstaining from inflicting any harm upon any being in any way (thought, word, and deed), at all times. It tells that if one does not practice total *ahimsa*, the practice of all the other *yamas* (disciplines) combined is worthless. *Ahimsa* is considered the highest *dharma* (virtue). *Ahimsa* has the capabilities of bonding all the other virtues together.

The *Yoga Sutras* direct one on a path to free oneself of attachment to the superficial aspects of the material world. They explain the human soul's oneness with all creation and with the Great Unknown. To achieve the state of enlightenment described within the *Yoga Sutras*, one must live guided by ethical principles. These principles include honesty, truthfulness, and nonviolence.[64] There are actually eight branches, or "limbs," within the philosophy of Yoga.[65, 66] These include:

THE EIGHT LIMBS OR BRANCHES OF THE PHILOSOPHY OF YOGA

   I. Disciplines *(Yamas)*
        Non-harming *(Ahimsa)*
        Truthfulness *(Satya)*
        Non-stealing *(Asteya)*
        Moderation of senses *(Brahmacharya)*
        Non-possessiveness *(Aparigrapha)*
  II. Observances *(Niyamas)*
        Purity *(Shaucha)*
        Contentment *(Santosha)*
        Self-discipline *(Tapas)*
        Self-study *(Svadhyaya)*
        Self-surrender *(Ishvara pranidhana)*
 III. Postures *(Asana)*[67, 68]
 IV. Breath Control *(Pranayama)*
  V. Introversion of Attention *(Pratyahara)*
 VI. Concentration *(Dharana)*
VII. Meditation *(Dhyana)*
VIII. Self-Realization *(Samadi)*

Living a life of *ahimsa* is of such importance in Yogic philosophy that the *Yoga Sutras* classify *himsa* (violence) into twenty-three levels of harm.[69] These levels are further classified according to the form of injury they cause, the intent behind the action (including all desires, anger, and ignorance), and the intensity of the harm that occurs. Only when one acts with the desire to live a life of total *ahimsa*, can one achieve the highest outcomes:

> *Therefore let everyone first examine well and then utter truth for*
> *the benefit of all living beings.*
>   *Surendranath Dasgupta*[70]

To fully adhere to the principles of Yoga, one must free oneself of superficial and impure thoughts. The methods (*Sadhana*) one uses to do so involve significant periods of concentration, deep levels of meditation, and sincere adherence to restraints. Nonviolence is the most crucial of these restraints—nonviolence toward all forms of life, at all times, in all places, and under all circumstances.[71]

The *Yoga Sutras* teach that once one recognizes the significance of nonviolence, one will seek to live adhering to it.

> *When there is natural firmness in non-violence all hostility comes*
> *to an end in its very presence.*
>
> *Yoga Sutras*[72]

Yoga Sutras foster cultivation of the habit of compassion towards all beings at all times. They teach that only by accepting total *ahimsa* in mind, speech, and action can one elevate one's consciousness to higher levels of understanding.[73]

> *[Ahimsa is] a great universal duty which a man should impose on*
> *himself in all conditions of life, everywhere, and at all times without*
> *restricting or qualifying it with limitations whatsoever.*
>
> *Yoga Sutras*[74]

The third branch of yoga, the exercises or *asanas*, represents that branch of Yoga that is well known within the Western world. The disciplines required in practicing the *asanas* guide one in the development of self-discipline. It is hoped that with such discipline, one will be better able to withdraw from the bonds of materiality so as to focus upon higher principles.

THE LAWS OF MANU

The *Laws of Manu* consist of ancient sacred teachings related to societal laws and personal conduct. Scholars believe they were written during the first or second century BCE. They embody principles inherent to Vedic philosophy. The details of their passages offer insight into how people lived and the principles they valued during India's ancient eras.[75] Because Brahmin priests passed these teachings down as literary traditions, they are considered religiously sanctioned traditions.[76]

The *Laws of Manu* are often described as one component within the set of works collectively referred to as the *Dharma Sutras*. These *Sutras* begin with an account of creation and continue further to describe rules of conduct to which each individual should adhere in his or her life. Though the term *dharma* generally refers to one's duty, in this situation it refers to moral and spiritual values that one should adhere to in one's heart.[77] The *Laws of Manu* are the most famous of the *Dharma Sutras*.

The rules of conduct within the *Laws of Manu* cover a wide range of topics attributed to an individual known as Manu. Linguistic studies relating to the metric nature of its verses indicate that it was probably formulated during the first or second century BCE. This was an era of ethical and spiritual transition. Though people observed Vedic rituals of sacrifice, they felt compassion for the animal being sacrificed.

THE TIRUKKURAL

The *Tirukkural* consists of a collection of South Indian spiritual and ethical teachings. They are sometimes referred to as the Tamil *Veda*. It has not been determined exactly when they were written; however, they were probably formulated sometime between the second century BCE and the eighth century CE. They contain numerous religious and philosophical principles that have guided the moral and ethical value system of Southeast India for centuries. Although they share much in common with the *Vedas*, they reject the caste system, deny the supremacy of the Brahmins, and condemn animal sacrifices.

The *Tirukkural* also contains many nonsectarian teachings often claimed by Brahmins, Jains, and Buddhists as their own. They teach that the highest virtue is that of not inflicting harm upon any being in thought, word, or action—at all times and without exception. According to the *Tirukkural*, not even the slightest distinction should be made as to whom the harm might be inflicted upon.[78]

> *If you ask what is the sum total of virtues, it is non-killing: killing begets sin.*
>
> *Tirukkural*[79]

THE PHILOSOPHY OF VEDANTA

The term Vedanta refers to the collection of religious-philosophical wisdom formulated by India's ancient philosophers based upon their analyses of the *Upanishads*, the *Brahma Sutra*, and the *Bhagavad Gita*.[80] The Philosophy of Vedanta places great value upon each of these sacred writings and believes that each corresponds to one of the spiritual stages within one's life. Experiencing these stages assists one to cultivate knowledge, faith, and discipline.

In Vedanta Philosophy, the *Upanishads* are viewed as the wisdom of sages, the *Brahma Sutras* viewed as writings clarifying and complementing the *Upanishads*, and the *Bhagavad Gita* as a guide to the inner journey one must follow to achieve Self-realization.[81]

Although Vedanta is a philosophy, it is well grounded within Hindu religious and spiritual values. It has often been described as a collection of interwoven threads of sacred religious thoughts, or a *Sutra*. These threads weave a pattern, or a tapestry, directing one to understand Hindu philosophical concepts, such as the ultimate meaning of the *Vedas*, the concept of God, and as the realization of the Self in all beings.[82]

The concepts that Vedanta analyzes are deeply spiritual and philosophical. Numerous philosophers have contributed to these philosophical interpretation. The philosophy of Vedanta analyzes Hindu philosophical concepts such as: the visible world being merely an illusion, the universal soul of God (*Brahman*) being a formless and eternal entity, and the soul of each individual (*Atman*) and the Soul of God (*Brahman*) being one and the same.

Vedanta teaches that each soul passes through a series of voyages within various beings, the fate of each has been determined by that soul's actions (*karma*) in its prior lives. Vedanta also discusses the concept that a unity exists between all things within the universe.[83]

There are several different philosophical perspectives within Vedanta. These include the perspectives of Sankara, Ramanuja and Madhva.[84] Their differences revolve around issues such as whether or not creation is the product of a Higher Source or, rather, of an unconscious flow of events, the relationship of *Brahman* (God) to all mind and matter, and the concept of whether or not all creation is a manifestation of the same God. In most perspectives, God is not simply an immanent Being in another realm. Rather, God is both transcendent and also present within each and every aspect of present-day life.[85]

Sankara's Philosophy of Vedanta, termed Advaita Vedanta, views the power of God and God as one and the same. He uses the analogy of the burning power of fire as being one with the fire itself. His analysis concludes that because all creation emanates from God, all is one with God.[86]

The existence of Brahman . . . [is the] . . . Self of every one. [87]

Advaita Vedanta teaches that because God is timeless, all existence is timeless. Hence, all creation is one with the past and the future—and all creation is one within God's continuous cycle of creation.

Foundational Concepts of the Hindu Faith

The Concept of God

Hinduism's Transition from Polytheism to Monotheism to Monism

Hinduism evolved as a faith over thousands of years. So too did the Hindu concept of God. Through analyses of the *Vedas* and other Hindu sacred scriptures, it has been recognized that Hinduism began as a faith based upon polytheism. It had been a faith immersed and entwined in beliefs in many different gods. Then it evolved into a faith with belief in one God that manifests in multiple forms without denying the existence of other deities (henotheism). Later, it evolved into a faith based upon the concept of one God (monotheism).

Eventually, Hinduism progressed even further. Sages began to recognize that God was not away and apart from all that God created. Accordingly, Hinduism evolved into a faith recognizing that all creation is one with God (monism).

The Hindu faith views God as being present in all. Because God is in all, God presents in a multitude of forms. Hence, God may reveal Itself in the form of many gods (*devas*). To one of Hindu faith, any one of these manifestations of God may be worshipped as a personal god. From the Vedic age forward, Hindus have believed in a unity of all gods. They do not deny any form through which God manifests or any form through which others perceive God.[88] Hence, they afford the highest respect to any and all forms through which God presents Itself to those of other faiths.

ALL CREATION IS A MANIFESTATION OF GOD

Hinduism teaches that all creation is a manifestation of God. The earliest *Veda*, the *Ṛg Veda*, and subsequent *Vedas*, teach that all existence — the heavens, planets, gods, earth, all living objects, and all non-living objects — are one with God. God pervades the world, yet remains beyond it. Because all creation is part of God, all that has ever been and all that will ever be are one.

> *The Man [God] had a thousand heads, a thousand eyes, a thousand feet: he covered the earth on all sides and stretched ten fingers' length beyond it. The Man was all that is and all that will be: ruling over immortality, He was all that grows by food.*
>
> *Ṛg Veda*[89]

In Hindu philosophy, the universe was created in, arose in, and remains in God. The universe, and all in it, will return to God. It is God, amidst the multitude of all that God has created, that the Hindu worships.[90] It is for this reason that Hinduism teaches respect for the essence of God within all beings. Based upon an understanding that God is in all, Hinduism considers the highest virtue to be nonviolence (*ahimsa*) toward all beings and all creation. All are God.[91] This concept of God being present within all creation has remained at the core of Hindu teachings for millennia.

> *All embodied life is in reality an incarnation of God . . . .*
>
> Mahatma Gandhi[92]

ALL CREATION IS OF ONE ESSENCE - INFINITELY

In Shankara's Hindu Philosophy of Vedanta, all aspects of existence that appear as differences between beings, objects, and even time, are mere illusions.

Brahman has in itself elements of manifoldness.[93]

In Hindu philosophical thought, all creation is integrally related within the cyclic continuum of infinite time and space. All creation exists within a continuous flow of recycling birth, life, and death. And, all will inevitably recycle back, again and again. New life could not be created were it not for the passing on of prior life. The future would not be born, were it not for the demise of the past. Based upon such beliefs, Hindus believe that all creation is one recycling essence. This "One" is God.

The Soul is the Same Soul in All Beings

In Hinduism, evolution is a cyclic, unified continuum. Similarly, the soul of each being is merely one entity cycling within this unified continuum. In Hindu philosophy, each being is perceived of as being composed of an outer cover, or envelope, and of an inner soul. One's envelope is merely a physical entity created to transport the soul.

The soul of each being does not vanish when its envelope, its body, dies. Rather, after a period of rest, the energy of that soul, including its unfulfilled desires, its fears, and its good and bad thoughts, words, and deeds, is passed on to reside within the envelope of yet another being. This cycle perpetuates itself—infinitely.

The soul of each being is merely a pinched off portion, likened to a wave of the ocean or a ray of the sun, from the Universal Soul—the Soul of God.

> *The past, the present and the future. . . all this, verily, is Brahman,*
> *but Brahman is this Atman (the soul).*
>
> *Mandukya Upanishad*[94]

A soul feels joy, pain, peace, and fear, just as does every other soul. When one soul suffers, all souls suffer. All souls possess the same emotional needs and sensitivities because all are of the same essence. All emanate from God. Eventually, just as all souls emanate from God, all souls will return to God.

> *Sages say this Self is infinite in the great and the small, everlasting*
> *and changeless, the source of all life.*
>
> *Mundaka Upanishad*[95]

GOD MANIFESTS IN AN INFINITE NUMBER OF FORMS

One beginning the study of Hinduism may wonder why there are so many gods. The various gods within the pantheon of Hindu gods are merely symbols of the various powers inherent within God's invisible Spirit. The gods are manifestations of God's creative, sustaining, and reclaiming force. This Force may have many names—God, Indra, Krishna, and Lord, yet all are perceived of as one essence.

In the *Bhagavad Gita*, Krishna, an avatar of Vishnu, the preserving aspect of God, speaks as the Soul of God, teaching Arjuna that God is present in every being.

> *My eternal seed, Arjuna, is to be found in every creature.*
> *Bhagavad Gita*[96]

The *Upanishads* explain that God controls and directs all. They tell that God is in the hearts of all, and that God is the final destiny to which all will return.

> *The Ruler is truly one; for the knowers of Brahman do not admit the*
> *existence of a second. He alone rules all the worlds by His powers.*
> *He dwells in the inner Self of every being. After having created all*
> *the worlds, He, their Protector, takes them back into Himself at the*
> *end of time.*
> *Shvetashvatara Upanishad*[97]

THE LAW OF KARMA

The *Law of Karma* is fundamental to Hindu thought. Though based upon somewhat different precepts, it is just as fundamental to Buddhist and Jain thought. The *Law of Karma* in all three of these faiths is much deeper, however, than the Western concept of, "As a man sows, so shall he reap."

The term *karma* refers both to one's actions and the results of one's actions. The *Law of Karma* places the responsibility for one's actions (one's *karma*) directly upon oneself. From a karmic perspective, one's "actions" include one's thoughts, words, and deeds. As one thinks, so will one act, and so will one become. One's actions will affect one's fate in the present life, and in all future lifetimes that one's soul will experience—infinitely until one is purified. One's actions also affect the fate of all other souls with whom one comes in contact. Recognition of the karmic effects of one's actions cannot help but lead one to strive to live a life of nonviolence.

Hinduism's *Law of Karma* (as differentiated from Buddhism's and Jainism's *Laws of Karma*) is founded upon the belief in a Universal Soul. The Universal Soul pervades all that exists, all that has ever existed, and all that will ever exist. Each being's soul emanates from the Universal Soul. The Universal Soul is eternal and immortal. Because each individual's soul emanates from the Universal Soul, each is eternal and immortal as well.

Human beings, however, cannot perceive the eternal nature of their souls because they are immersed in the material world. In the *Bhagavad Gita*, Krishna tells Arjuna that although we have forgotten the sins or good deeds that each of us has set in motion during our present or our prior lifetimes, God remembers all!

> *You and I have passed through many births, Arjuna. You have forgotten, but I remember them all.*
>
> *Bhagavad Gita*[98]

To one of Hindu faith, all souls are perceived as possessing an inherent desire to return to the Universal Soul. This desire is termed salvation or *Moksha*. During each soul's passage through its present lifetime, if it performs impure actions (creates negative *karma*), that soul must purify itself before it can return to the Universal Soul.[99]

Because it is so difficult to live a perfect life, souls cannot easily return to the Universal Soul. Therefore, they generally enmesh in a continuous round of rebirths. This cycling of each soul within different beings is termed *Samsara*.

Some Hindu philosophers state that the individual's soul, its *atman*, always remains pure and is only shrouded by negative *karma*. One can peel off these layers or shrouds of *karma* through atonement, through austerities (*tapas*), through meditation, and through the guidance of a sage, or guru, who is personally free of *karma*.

One's actions will determine one's fate in present and future lifetimes. One's soul may not necessarily return in human form in its next lifetime.[100] The fate each soul experiences in various lifetimes is totally dependent upon the individual's past actions.[101]

Hence, Hinduism's *Law of Karma* includes three interrelated components: *Karma*—the future of all existence depends upon one's actions; *Samsara*—the eternal cycle of transmigration of one's soul into future beings; and *Moksha*—salvation or joining with the Universal Soul. *Karma* is the determining factor for all.[102]

The concept that one's actions have perpetual repercussions, is similar to the Western theory termed the "Butterfly Effect." In 1963, Lorenz demonstrated that the simple flapping of a butterfly's wings in Madagascar would alter the course of weather on our planet forever. Lorenz calculated that the number of effects emanating from each and every action disseminates concentrically and increases exponentially from the source of the action. As effects interact with one another, the course of the future is modified—infinitely.[103]

According to the Hindu *Law of Karma*, all that occurs does so as a result of both the personal and the collective *karma* of all others.

Though one cannot normally recall what has occurred in one's prior existences, God remembers all! God directs one's future according to the course one's soul chose to pursue in its past and present lives. The *Law of Karma* is neither fatalistic nor pessimistic. Each individual has the opportunity to create a better life for an infinite number of beings, now and forever.

> *Those who work in the service of the Lord are free from the law of*
> *Karma.*
>
> *Shvetashvatara Upanishad[104]*

THE LAW OF REBIRTH

The Hindu *Law of Rebirth* is inextricably intertwined with the Hindu *Law of Karma*. To understand both the *Law of Karma* and the *Law of Rebirth*, one must first understand Hinduism's concept of the soul.

In Hindu philosophy, a soul exists within each being. Each soul emanates from, and is part of, the Universal Soul—the Soul that has always permeated all existence. The *Law of Rebirth* teaches that each soul is reborn again and again into a series of lives. The challenges that each soul must face are determined by its actions in prior lives. Accordingly, the actions it performs during its present life affect the fate it will encounter in its future lives.[105]

Recognizing this, a Hindu feels sympathy with all beings facing challenges, human and non-human. They recognize that each and every being is bound within its own eternal continuum, yet all are part of the Universal Soul.

> *There is one all-pervading Atman (Self). It is the innermost soul of all beings. If you injure your neighbor, you really injure yourself. If you injure any other creature, you really injure yourself, because the whole world is really nothing but yourself.*[106]

One who recognizes that one's soul is intertwined with the souls of all other beings, will act for the betterment of all. Only the soul of one who has lived with total purity can escape the cycle of rebirths (*samsara*) to become one with the Universal God.

> *When one attains the supreme Brahman which is unborn, unchangeable, undecaying, immortal, fearless, eternal, self-luminous, all-blissful, and all-pervading—one is freed from births and deaths.*
> *Isavasya Upanishad*[107]

Understanding the *Laws of Karma* and *Rebirth*, Hindus recognize that in one way or another, and in one lifetime or another, one must experience the effects of one's prior actions.

> *The Self is born again and again in new bodies to work out the karma of future lives. The embodied self assumes many forms, heavy or light, according to its needs for growth and for the deeds of previous lives. This evolution is a divine law.*
> *Shvetashvatara Upanishad*[108]

EVOLUTION TOWARD VEGETARIANISM—FROM SACRIFICE TO SANCTITY

To understand Hinduism's philosophy of nonviolence, one must first understand the evolution of these values. Hinduism evolved from an ancient belief system involved in animal sacrifice to gods, to one with deep reverence toward the God in all beings. The following passages explain this transition.

ANIMAL SACRIFICE IN EARLY HINDUISM

During Vedic times, the god Indra was perceived as an all-powerful deity—a deity dominating the universe. It was predominantly to Indra, this all-pervading deity, that the people of India offered sacrifices. They perceived both the bright sun in the sky and fire upon earth as symbols of Indra. Accordingly, they worshipped Indra through the sun in the heavens and through the fire upon earth. They believed that all vegetation and animals consumed by sacrificial fires would reach the deity in whose name they were offered.[109]

> *Herbs, trees, cattle, birds, and (other) animals that have been destroyed for sacrifices, receive (being reborn) higher existences.*
> *Laws of Manu*[110]

Ancient writings of this era, predominantly the writings of the *Ṛg Veda*, contain historical accounts of such rituals. They also contain insight into the prayers of its followers and of their longings to attain the mercy and assistance of a Higher Power.

One of the people's most pressing concerns had been control of the unpredictable course of nature. In an attempt to combat drought, famine, plagues, and other natural catastrophes, people performed rituals, issued holy words, utterances, prayers, and invocations. They also sacrificed plants and animals. Numerous passages of the *Brahmanas* of the *Vedas* deal with rituals of animal sacrifice.

Within these early civilizations, animal sacrifices were not considered acts of violence. Rather, they were considered acts of benevolence, as it was believed that those animals being sacrificed would attain an elevated status in future lives. They also believed that by performing sacrifices, the rest of the community would be protected.

> *Know this Fire to be the means of attaining Heaven.*
> *Katha Upanishad*[111]

One of the most well known sacrifices described within the *Brahmanas* is the horse-sacrifice, the *asvamedha* sacrifice. A designated horse was set free for one year. It was followed and at the end of that year, the chieftain upon whose lands the horse wandered was required to pay a fee. If he refused to pay, he was required to fight the people who set the horse free. However, if at the end of that year the horse was not on anyone's land, it was sacrificed.[112]

A description of the sacrifice taken from perhaps the oldest *Upanishad,* the *Brihadaranyaka* – the *Great Forest Text*, explains that the anatomic parts of the horse represented specific regions of the cosmos. The horse's eye was perceived as the sun, his back as the sky, and his abdomen as the earth. The sacrificial altar was perceived as representing matter and liquid—the basic elements from which all creation emerged.[113] Followers of this tradition believed that performing the ritual sacrifice, along with meditation, would help one understand the meaning of life and of the universe.[114]

> *One may eat meat when it has been sprinkled with water, while*
> *Mantras were recited . . . when one is engaged (in the performance*
> *of a rite) according to the law.*
> *Laws of Manu*[115]

40

QUESTIONING ANIMAL SACRIFICE

With time, however, people began to question the Vedic sacrifices. The *Bhagavata Purana* was one of Hinduism's earliest writings questioning animal sacrifice. It states that animal sacrifice is not useful and advises people that instead of performing animal sacrifices, one should look within oneself for spiritual understanding.

> *Leaving the ritualistic way let your mind on restraint proceed. Living in a quiet place on meager food ... [practice] nonviolence. [He who] worships God with purity of mind and performs austerities will attain success.*
>
> *Bhagavata Purana*[116]

The *Varaha Purana* advises that those who take joy in any act of violence, including sacrifice, are cruel, and that they create obstacles to the furtherance of good. Even acts such as destroying green grass, killing buffaloes and goats, and setting forest fires are considered evil.[117]

> *Those engaged in various deeds following Vedic principles though the deeds are not hateful ... such people so waste their earthly lives and never gain God's blessing and grace.*
>
> *Bhagavata Purana*[118]

Over time, writings such as the *Bhagavad Gita* have been advising people that those who see God everywhere, need not look to the rules of ancient cultures to attain communion with God.

> *Just as a reservoir is of little use when the whole countryside is flooded, scriptures are of little use to the illuminated man or woman who sees the Lord everywhere.*
>
> *Bhagavad Gita*[119]

The *Puranas* begin to teach that living a life of *ahimsa*, nonviolence, is of greater value than performing sacrifices. They tell that a virtuous individual will act with equal benevolence toward all.[120] The *Bhagavata Purana* teaches:

> *Whoever listens to righteous words and understands their essence will never perform ancestors' 'Sradha' [sacrifices] with offerings of animal flesh . . . [or] stoop to killing of animals . . . [or] torture animals either in mind, word, or deed.*
>
> *Bhagavata Purana*[121]

Some believe that the ancient Hindu concern for weaker beings, particularly the cow, originated purely for economic reasons. They theorize that the cow, as a supplier of milk, as a beast of burden, and as a supplier of future cows was protected because it was more valuable alive than when slaughtered. Such a theory, however, does not answer the question as to why ancient Hindu writings indicate that injured, disabled, and defective cows (cows with only three legs, cows that were emaciated, and bulls too feeble to pull plows) were protected. It also does not explain why they were considered holy.[122]

By the sixth century BCE, when the futility of animal sacrifice had become obvious, people began to value practices of nonviolence and vegetarianism. Some researchers believe this transition was merely a natural course of evolution. Yet this transition did not occur in other lands.[123]

Actually, this was an era of great spiritual transition. Many people had begun to hold *ahimsa* as their most sacred value. Members of the Indus Valley civilization began to practice meditation and pacifism toward animals. As these practices gained recognition, traditional Brahmanic practices of sacrifice were set aside.

> *Eastern India saw the rise of a class of wandering teachers who, though believing in the doctrine of transmigration and Karma, rejected the authority of the Vedas and of vedic priests, denounced the bloody sacrifices that constituted so large a part of the Brahmanic ritual and even denied the existence of God and consequently the efficacy of divine grace. Right conduct, they declared, was the way of getting out of the meshes of Karma and Samsara, and this right conduct included, among other things, the practice of Ahimsa, or noninjury to living beings.*
>
> Majumdar[124]

Concepts of *ahimsa* and vegetarianism spread across India. Brahmanic priests, those who held rights to sacrifice animals, became the staunchest advocates of nonviolence.

> *The prohibition of flesh, which became increasingly strict in brah-manic society, was one way to break the chain of all this alimentary violence and affirm that it is not really necessary to kill in order to eat. To that end, a new type of opposition between men was intro-duced. It was no longer a matter of courage and fear, domination and servitude; it was instead an opposition between the pure and the impure. Abstention from eating meat became a criterion of pu-rity.*
>
> Zimmerman[125]

The *Laws of Manu* tell that although the taking of an animal's life for religious reasons may have been meritorious, abstinence from meat was equally holy.

> *He who during a hundred years annually offers a horse-sacrifice, and he who entirely abstains from meat, obtain the same reward for their meritorious (conduct).*
>
> *Laws of Manu*[126]

Over the passage of time, the practice of animal sacrifice began to arouse the consciences of many.

> *We use no sacrificial stake. We slay no victims. We worship en-tirely by the repetition of the sacred verses.*
>
> *Sama Veda*[127]

The ancient writings of the *Tirukkural*, the teachings of South India sometimes referred to as the *Tamil Veda*, voice strong opposition to animal sacrifice. They assert that the highest virtue is abstaining from inflicting harm upon others in thought, word, or action—at all times and without exception. They state that no distinction should be made as to whom the harm will affect—as no one should be harmed.[128] In a chapter concerning ingestion of flesh, the *Tirukkural* states

> *The meat eater cannot really practice mercy.*
> *Tirukkural*[129]

The *Tirukkural* tells that it is better to save the life of one being and to abstain from consumption of its flesh than to perform a thousand sacrifices.

> *Better than a thousand burnt offerings is one life unkilled, uneaten.*
> *Tirukkural*[130]

Passages of the *Upanishads* reveal that many had begun to undergo mental and spiritual conversions away from ritual sacrifice, and towards deeper internal spiritual understanding.

> *Unsteady, verily, are these boats of the eighteen sacrificial forms,*
> *which are said to be inferior karma. The deluded who delight in this*
> *as leading to good, fall again into old age and death.*
> *Mundaka Upanishad*[131]

The *Mundaka Upanishad* came to the conclusion that animal sacrifice was ineffectual as a means of attaining spiritual grace, stating that it incorrectly substituted material and worldly sacrifice for more meaningful inward, spiritual sacrifice.[132]

> *The immature, living manifoldly in ignorance, think 'we have accomplished our aim.' Those who perform rituals do not understand (the truth).*
>
> Mundaka Upanishad[133]

Over generations, the misguided nature of animal sacrifice became recognized. Accordingly, its practice gradually diminished. Sages began to teach that the highest sacrifice was that performed within oneself. Recognizing the value of personal sacrifice, many Hindus recognized the shallowness of material possessions and retired into hermitages to follow lives of meditation and prayer.[134]

MOVEMENT TOWARD ANIMAL PROTECTION

Even during Vedic times, the *Artha Sastra*, a fourth century text devoted to the functioning of the state, tells that herds of aged, diseased, and sterile cattle were being kept alive. This indicates that in some regions, cattle were permitted to live a natural lifespan and die of natural causes.[135] By the time the *Upanishads* were written, nonviolence toward all beings had already become a valued concept. Combining Hindu teachings with those of Buddhists and Jains, the gradual transition away from animal sacrifice was inevitable.

Ritual animal sacrifice met its final days, in large part, due to the dissemination of Buddhist concepts within India. During the third century BCE, the Mauryan Dynasty conquered almost the entire subcontinent of India. The leader's grandson, Emperor Asoka (c. 274-232 BCE) ascended the throne. Though raised a Hindu, Emperor Asoka converted to Buddhism, enforced values of nonviolence, and prohibited sacrifice throughout the nation.

Such values became so ingrained within Indian society that by the early fifth century CE, no Indian of respectable caste consumed meat. Apparently, even during these ancient eras, people of higher castes were vegetarian. Vedic principles of nonviolence had become so deeply established, that the evolution toward vegetarianism was inevitable.[136]

MOVEMENT TOWARD AHIMSA

Ahimsa is a Sanskrit word meaning harmlessness, abstaining from causing pain to another. It represents the highest virtue within Hindu philosophy. It includes non-injury in thought, word and deed toward any and all beings.[137] Concepts of nonviolence have endured for generations throughout India.

> *Do not commit any act of violence though your life is in peril.*
> *Tirukkural[138]*

The Hindu concept of *ahimsa* includes never harming or killing any being either physically or by thinking negative thoughts about that being. One must sacrifice one's own self for the welfare of all others, must feel love for the entirety of creation, and must resist revenge upon a wrong doer.

> *Non-injuring in thought, word and deed is the highest of all virtues.*
> Swami Sivananda[139]

MOVEMENT TOWARD SANCTIFICATION OF THE COW

Much understanding of the true meanings of ancient Hindu scriptures has been lost. Yet some passages of the *Ṛg Veda* seem to indicate that the cow was not only highly valued, but that it was sometimes equated with God. *Samhitas* of several *Vedas* express great reverence for the cow. They tell that acts of cruelty toward cows spiritually weaken the individual committing such acts. Some express foreboding message that those who act with cruelty toward a cow will face a miserable death and may be sent to hell. One *Samhita* forbids any acts of cruelty toward cows.

> *Whoever hurts, or causes another to hurt, steals, or causes to*
> *steal, a cow should be slain.*
> *Brahat Prasara Samhita*[140]

A number of local folk tales reveal that values of nonviolence had begun to spread with great fervor throughout India. One legend has it that King Chola ordered the execution of his son for accidentally killing a cow. Another, the tale of Kumarapala (c. 1143–1172), tells of a Gujarat Jain king who so strictly enforced nonviolence that he even levied fines against those who killed fleas. Although such stories may be mere legend, they shed insight into the value placed upon nonviolence. Within some regions of India, the wanton killing of cows became one of the most serious crimes.[141]

Some believe such reverence arose because the cow has always given so much to humanity as a source of milk and as a beast of burden. Some believe it is because the cow's serenity exemplifies universal peace. Others hypothesize that because of its giving nature, the cow may have been a symbol of motherhood.[142] Looking beyond hypotheses, the fact remains that reverence for the cow became a respected value amongst the Hindus of India.

An indication of the values placed upon cows became apparent in 1966, when 100,000 persons marched on the parliament in New Delhi seeking a national ban on the slaughter of cows.[143] Mahatma Gandhi considered the sanctity of the cow as a symbol of humankind's indissoluble relationship with non-human beings.[144] To one of Hindu faith, the salvation of humankind depends upon all doing their share in upholding truth and nonviolence.[145]

The Buddhist Faith

Origins

[A man is noble if] he has pity on all living creatures.

Dammapada[146]

An understanding of Buddhism, and of the mutual effects Buddhism and Hinduism had upon each other, is necessary to understand the evolution of vegetarian values within India. Although Buddhism ceased to exist as a major tradition within India by 1200 CE, the seventeen hundred years during which Hinduism and Buddhism mutually coexisted greatly affected India's culture.[147]

Some believe that the main reason Buddhism declined within India was not because it was suppressed by foreign conquerors, but because it was merged into Hinduism. Even from its inception, Buddhism was never entirely isolated from Hinduism. Because a foundational concept within Hinduism is reverence for all faiths, many Hindus integrated Buddhist philosophy into their own personal belief systems.

By 400 CE, millions of Hindus incorporated Buddha into their religion, considering him an avatar (a reincarnation) of Vishnu.[148] Buddha was worshiped in many Hindu shrines as a god; Buddhist monks and Hindu priests joined together in religious events; and many Buddhist sages were incorporated into the Hindu pantheon of deities. Aspects of Buddhist philosophy were incorporated into the Hindu Philosophy of Vedanta. Similarly, the Hindu Vaishnavas sect incorporated Buddhist teachings into its own teachings. Hence, although Buddhism was absorbed into Hinduism, Buddhism left an indelible mark upon Hinduism.[149]

Similarly, many Buddhist concepts of *ahimsa* had been founded, at least in part, upon ancient Hindu Brahmanas.[150] Although Hinduism originated in Northwestern India, and Jainism and Buddhism in Eastern India, over generations, people of all faiths seemed to merge many of their beliefs.[151] Through assimilation, Buddhism was gradually absorbed into the Hindu faith.[152]

GAUTAMA BUDDHA

The Buddha was born Gautama Siddhartha, the son of a Hindu chieftan of a hill tribe of the Shakyas, in present-day southern Nepal. During most of his life, he lived and taught along the banks of the Ganges River. He believed that each individual must forge his or her own personal path to attain inner peace. He taught that only one who lives a life of nonviolence will attain peace, and only if all people live in nonviolence will the world attain peace. His philosophy spread from eastern India as Theravedic Buddhism to western India, where Mahayana Buddhism took form. From there it spread to southeast Asia and parts of Japan. Subsequently, his teachings spread from western India to China, Korea, and, also, parts of Japan.

Buddha taught of a lifestyle devoid of harming or killing any human or nonhuman being.[153] He believed that all existence, all life, and all beings, were related, and that any perception of differences was mere illusion. The ancient Buddhist Pali Canon tells that if one leads a life of right thought, speech, and deed, one will avoid harming any being.[154]

ORIGIN AND SPREAD OF THE BUDDHIST FAITH

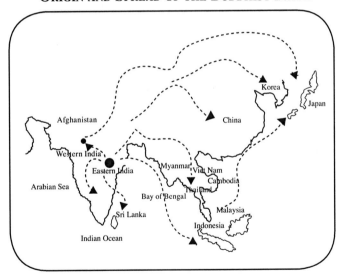

Adapted from Ninian Smart, *Atlas of World Religions*, 24-25.[155]

SACRED TEACHINGS

THE DHAMMAPADA

Three months after Gautama Buddha's death, his followers assembled and collected his teachings, the *Dhammapada*, "The Footsteps of Religion." *Dhamma* refers to the virtues taught by the Buddha, and *Pada* means place, protection, or footstep. Hence, the term *Dhammapada* refers to the path, or footsteps, one should take to lead a virtuous life.[156]

> *He who, by causing pain to others, wishes to obtain pleasure for himself, he entangles in the bands of hatred, will never be free from hatred.*
>
> Dhammapada[157]

The *Dhammapada* contains four hundred and twenty-three concepts that Buddha shared over forty-five years of teaching. He expressed these on various levels so that various listeners might best understand them.[158] By the first century BCE, Buddha's teachings were reduced to writing. The *Dhammapada* explains that all beings possess the same longing for peace, freedom, and life, as do all other beings. No individual should rob any being of these.[159]

> *All men tremble at punishment, all men love life; remember that thou art like unto them, and do not kill, nor cause slaughter.*
>
> Dhammapada[160]

One section of the *Dhammapada*, the *Mettasutta* tells of Buddha's concern that goodwill and peace be extended toward all beings:

> *Whatever living beings there are, whether feeble or strong, either long or great, middle-sized, short, small or large, either seen or which are not seen, and which live far (or) near, either born or seeking birth, may all creatures be happy-minded. Let no one deceive another, let him not despise (another) in any place, let him not out of anger or resentment wish harm to another. And let him cultivate goodwill towards all the world, a boundless (friendly) mind above and below and across, unobstructed, without hatred, without enmity.*
>
> *Mettasutta*[161]

The first vow a Buddhist monk must take is the vow of vegetarianism. In many Buddhist communities, this means a total commitment to vegetarianism. In others, it means that monks may eat meat if the animal had not been killed for their benefit. The tenth vow of a Buddhist monk is that of nonviolence toward any weaker being. In this vow, monks are advised to use a cloth to strain drinking water (as do holy individuals of the Jain faith) so as not to take the life of any unseen life forms living within the water.[162]

SUTTA-NIPATA

The *Sutta-Nipata* is a collection of early Buddhist discourses. Its purpose is to guide one to attain inner peace and tranquility. To achieve these, one must feel compassion for all living beings.[163] In these, Buddha tells that one who does not harm other beings is holy.

> *Whosoever, after refraining from hurting (living) creatures, (both) those that tremble and those that are strong, does not kill or cause to be killed. Him I call a Brahmana [Brahmin priest].*
>
> *Sutta-Nipata*[164]

Buddha believed that the original creators of Hinduism did not intend to include animal sacrifice. He felt that this crept into the religion slowly due to misguided beliefs.

> *[Brahmin priests] They give food, and they give strength, they likewise give (a good) complexion and happiness; knowing the real state of this, they did not kill cows.*
>
> *Sutta-Nipata*[165]

THE LANKAVATARA SUTRA

Buddhist teachings within the *Lankavatara Sutra* guide people to look upon all beings with compassion and kindness.

> *Wherever living beings evolve, men should feel toward them as to their own kin, and, looking on all beings as their own child should refrain from eating meat.*
>
> *Lankavatara Sutra*[166]

The Wisdom of Emperor Asoka

During the third century BCE, the Greeks, led by Alexander the Great, invaded Western India. In 323 BCE when Alexander died, an Indian leader, Chandragupta Maurya, drove the Greek forces out of India. Maurya was able to unify the entire continent of India, except for the southern tip, under his rule, forming the Mauryan Empire.

Emperor Maurya's grandson, Emperor Asoka (c.274-232 BCE) assumed leadership of the empire. Emperor Asoka had been raised a Hindu. After recognizing the suffering he inflicted upon others by the war he had been forced to wage, he felt tremendous remorse. He wrote of this by carving edicts on rocks, pillars, and caves throughout India.

> *[Emperor Asoka] is moved to remorse now. For he has felt profound sorrow and regret because the conquest of a people previously unconquered involves slaughter, death, and deportation.*
> Rock Edict XIII[167]

Emperor Asoka experienced a spiritual conversion and became a Buddhist. He declared animal sacrifices illegal throughout the entire Empire, promoted vegetarianism, prohibited consumption of meat at the royal table, and fostered peace and nonviolence.

> *[All] suffer from the injury, slaughter, and deportation of their loved ones. . . . Therefore, even if the number of people who were killed or who died or who were carried away in the Kalinga war had been only one-hundredth or one-thousandth of what it actually was, this still would have weighed on the king's mind.*
> Rock Edict XIII[168]

Under his reign, Emperor Asoka spread Buddhism throughout all of India.[169] He had become so holy that many believe he took vows to become a Buddhist monk.[170] He referred to his carved inscriptions as records of morality he had chosen to follow, that he hoped would endure for generations to come.[171] He carved the inscription of Rock Edict XIII so that future generations might not seek further conquests.[172]

This edict on Dharma has been inscribed so that my sons and great-grandsons who may come after me should not think new conquests worth achieving. If they do conquer, let them take pleasure in moderation and mild punishments. Let them consider moral conquest the only true conquest.

Rock Edict XIII[173]

The carved inscriptions of Emperor Asoka are actually the earliest legible written records to have survived upon the continent of India. His teachings disseminated humane values throughout the entire nation of India.

I have decreed many kindnesses, including even the grant of life, to living creatures, two-footed and four-footed as well as birds and aquatic animals.

Pillar Edict II[174]

During Asoka's reign, he abandoned aggression toward all other countries, claiming that through peaceful practices and humanitarian leadership, he had won many victories.[175] During his reign, Buddhism grew from a small Indian sect to a nationwide philosophy. The essence of his philosophy of nonviolence is summed up in this tiny sentence.

No living creature shall be slaughtered here.

Rock Edict I[176]

After the reign of Emperor Asoka, other leaders of India followed similar philosophies of nonviolence and vegetarianism. The Gupta family was a family of wealthy landowners who, in c. 320 CE, secured control of India. Their kingdom centered near the Ganges River, and its borders extended from one coast of India to the other. Gupta kings made large endowments to both Buddhist and Hindu religious communities, and facilitated the spread of nonviolence across the continent.[177] By this time, animal sacrifice was no longer practiced within India. It had been replaced by practices of inner spirituality and practices of compassion toward all beings.

In 460 CE, foreign invaders conquered the Gupta Empire. For more than a century, India was under foreign rule.[178] Finally a Hindu, Emperor Harsha (606—647 CE), regained control of Northern India. Emperor Harsha held great reverence for both Hindu and Buddhist principles, and spread values of nonviolence and vegetarianism throughout his entire kingdom. A Chinese pilgrim traveling through India at that time, wrote

> *[The Emperor Harasha] caused the use of animal food to cease throughout his dominions and prohibited the taking of life.[179]*

In summary, Buddhism had a profound effect upon the social, philosophical, and spiritual soul of India. Though the number of Buddhists within India declined, the effects of Buddhist philosophy certainly has not. Buddhist concepts became absorbed within Hinduism, and left an indelible legacy advancing nonviolence and vegetarianism within the entire continent of India.

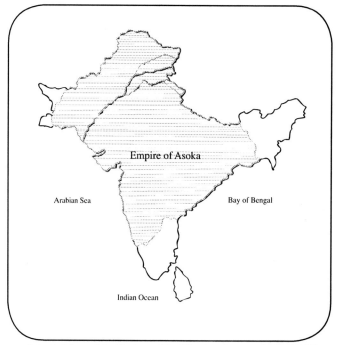

Adapted from A.L. Basham, *The Wonder that was India*, 52.[180]

THE JAIN FAITH

ORIGINS

The Jain faith holds nonviolence toward all beings as its highest goal. Jain practices of austerity and self-sacrifice evolved over centuries to prevent the infliction of harm upon any weaker beings. Jain practices of nonviolence are of such depth and such commitment that they have strengthened the cause of nonviolence throughout all India.

Historians cannot determine exactly when the Jain faith originated. Some scholars believe that some aspects of Jain teachings may have emerged as early as the ninth century BCE. Others believe Jain teachings originated as a distinct entity only 2,500 years ago. The Jain faith, however, can be traced back with historical accuracy to approximately 850 BCE.

Some believe that Neminatha, a contemporary of Krishna, may have founded the Jain faith.[181] The prevalent belief, however, is that spiritual guides, termed *tirthankara*, have appeared upon the earth within specified time cycles.[182] Twenty-four such spiritual guides are recognized, and each has rekindled the Jain faith.

Parsava was the twenty-third Jain spiritual teacher. He lived in Varanasi (formerly Banaras) and taught along the banks of the Ganges River.[183] He enjoined his followers to follow four great vows: *ahimsa* (not injuring), *satya* (truthfulness), *asteya* (not stealing), and *aparigraha* (nonpossessiveness of property). Of these vows, *ahimsa* is considered of greatest importance.[184]

Mahavira, 599 BCE to 527 BCE, is the most recent Jain spiritual teacher. Born two hundred and fifty years after the death of Parsava, and as the twenty-fourth Jain *tirthankara*, Mahavira amassed over 500,000 followers in the ways of Jain teachings such as

> *Every creature and every being suffers pain and is afflicted. Doing harm to these beings, an ignorant man becomes involved in sins.*
>
> *Sutrakritanga*[185]

The term "Jain" comes from the root "*ji*" (to conquer), to conquer one's own emotions and physical cravings. During ancient times, Jains were opposed to the Vedic ritual of sacrifice. They felt that all beings possessed value, and each and every being should be protected.[186]

Jains follow a canon of literature known as the *Siddhanta* (also known as the *Nigantha-pavayana* sermons). This canon of sixty texts is divided into three groups.[187] Jains do not view their teachings as having been revealed through divine revelation as Hindus view the *Vedas*. Rather, the Jains view the *Siddhanta* as truths an individual's soul comes to know.

Since the origination of the faith, almost all Jain sects have always advocated *ahimsa* (nonviolence) toward all beings. Nonviolence is an unconditional moral doctrine, and vegetarianism has been one of the most tangible expressions of this doctrine.[188] Jains feel that every form of life is of value. They categorize all beings into forms; the lowest form is termed a nigoda. Nigodas are those minute life forms that are so undifferentiated that they do not contain a body that is visible to the naked eye. They live together in clusters, surviving only a fleeting moment.

The next higher form of beings are earth, water, fire, and air bodies. They possess only one sense, the sense of touch. The highest form of beings are plants and animals. Jains have analyzed all life forms, including worms, flies, and serpents. All are of value. To a Jain, all life is meaningful, even insects in dung, organisms in water, and bacteria in liquid. Even the humblest of beings must be respected.

> *Grass, trees, and plants, and all creatures that move. . . these are*
> *classes of living beings. Know that they all seek happiness.*
> *Sutrakṛtanga*[189]

In the Jain faith, *karma* is perceived as a physical entity that adheres to one's body. *Karma* can be positive or negative—causing harm and preventing harm. Some forms of *karma* inflict one with a sense of delusion, and obstruct one from recognizing truth.

> *There is nothing mightier in the world than karma; karma tramples down all powers, as an elephant a clump of lotuses.*
> *Bhagavati Aradhana*[190]

If one's soul is not pure, and one's passions are not calmed, negative *karma* will stick to one's soul—just as moist soil sticks when thrown at a wall. Jains seek to escape the difficult cycle of life, death, and rebirth, by not gaining new negative *karma* and by eliminating residues of negative *karma* from previous lifetimes.[191] Only one born as a human, having the capacity to reason and to sense the plight of others, can eliminate *karma*.[192]

> *As it would be unto thee, so it is with him whom thou intendest to kill. The righteous man who lives with these sentiments, does therefore neither kill nor cause others to kill (living beings).*
> *Akaranga Sutra*[193]

SACRED TEACHINGS

Jain sacred teachings, the *Siddhanta*, were codified two hundred years after Mahavira's death, and finalized by the fifth century CE. There are three components to the *Siddhanta*: the *Purvas*, *Angas*, and *Angabahyas*. The *Purvas* contain ancient teachings on astrology, astronomy, and the soul. Only brief fragments of the *Purvas* remain. The *Angas* teach lifestyles that nuns and monks must follow to avoid inflicting injury upon even the most minute forms of life.[194] The *Angabahyas* teach lifestyles that each Jain layperson must follow so as to live without harming any being.

> *Whatever beings there are, whether moving or non-moving, thou shall not hurt, whether knowingly or unknowingly . . . All beings desire to live; no one wants to die. Therefore a nirgantha refrains from all acts of injury.*
>
> *Dasavaikalika-sutra*[195]

Jains place the responsibility for an individual's fate not in the hands of a god, but rather in the hands of that individual.

> *Oh man, refrain from evil, for life must come to an end. Only foolish men and [the] uncontrolled are plunged into the habit of pleasure. Living in striving and self-control, for hard to cross are paths full of insects. Heroes, detached and strenuous, subduing anger and fear, will never kill living beings, but cease from sin and are happy.*
>
> *Sutrakṛtanga*[196]

Because Jains view their soul as existing within a realm of recycling bondage, they identify with the soul of each being trapped within its own cycle. Accordingly, one of Jain faith feels kinship and compassion with all other beings.[197]

> *The world is boundless and eternal, it exists from eternity and does not perish.*
>
> *Sutrakritanga*[198]

PHILOSOPHY OF THE JAIN FAITH

Within the Jain faith, *ahimsa* means never hurting the "life-principle" of any other be-ing—either physically or mentally. To Jains, it is worse if one harms another motivated by conscious intent than if one harms another accidentally. Because each life represents a segment within the continuity of all life, Jains believe that humans must strive to help every other being. Killing any being constitutes a terrible action not just for that being, but even more so for the perpetrator. For the perpetrator is held within the grips of a tormenting karmic cycle of rebirths.[199]

> *Whatever cruelty he has done in a former birth, the same will be inflicted on him in a Circle of Births. Having been born in an extremely miserable state of life, the sufferer experiences infinite pain.*
>
> *Sutrakritanga*[200]

Jains believe that to gain salvation, one must not even tread accidentally upon an insect that crosses one's path.

> *To do harm to others is to do harm to oneself. "Thou art he whom thou intendest to kill. Thou art he whom thou intendest to tyrannize over!" We corrupt ourselves as soon as we intend to corrupt others. We kill ourselves as soon as we intend to kill others.*
>
> *Acaranga Sutra*[201]

The most serious sin in the Jain faith is to injure another being. This includes any being liv-ing in water, fire, earth, or wind; all plants; all those born of eggs (birds), all born of fetus (elephants), all born from an enveloping membrane (cows), all born from fluids (worms), all born from sweat (insects), all born by coagulation (locust), all born from cocoons (but-terflies), and all born by regeneration (men, gods, hell-beings).[202] The passion for *ahimsa* is so strong that a Jain refrains from all thoughts and speech that might lead to the harming of another being.[203]

It is obvious that with such strong principles concerning not killing, that Jains would object to the consumption of animal flesh—as this is integrally related to the taking of the animal's life. Going one step further, Jains often avoid sweet and fermented foods, including alcohol, honey, sweet and fleshy foods, and also some plants with seeds, because these may contain many minute life forms, nigodas.[204] The first vow of Mahavira's five great vows expresses this commitment:

> *I renounce all killing of living beings, whether subtle or gross,*
> *whether movable or immovable. Nor shall I myself kill living beings*
> *(nor cause others to do it, nor consent to it).*
>
> *Akaranga Sutra*[205]

The Jain philosophy of nonviolence finds its full expression during India's four-month monsoon season. During this season, plant and insect life flourishes. To avoid walking on and injuring these life forms, Jains are extremely cautious. They remain indoors to avoid stepping on insects. They gently brush the ground ahead of them when they must venture outdoors.[206]

A Jain monk seeks to control his actions, mind, and speech lest these might lead to subtle acts of violence. He even takes care where he places his alms bowl and inspects his food and drink to ensure they do not contain any minute life forms.

> *When the rainy season has come . . . many living things are origi-*
> *nated and many seeds just spring up . . . Knowing this one should*
> *not wander from village to village, but stay in one place during the*
> *rainy season.*
>
> *Akaranga Sutra*[207]

In summary, the Jain contribution to the philosophy of nonviolence amongst the populace of India has been profound.[208] Mahatma Gandhi grew up in the Gujarat region of India, where many people of the Jain faith live. Though his family was of Hindu Vaishnavas sect, Gandhi recognized the profound effect the Jain faith had upon their lives.

> *The Gandhis were Vaishnavas . . . Jainism was strong in Gujarat, and its influence was felt everywhere and on all occasions. The opposition to and the abhorrence of meat-eating that existed in Gujarat among the Jains and Vaishnavas were to be seen nowhere else in India or outside in such strength. These were the traditions in which I was born and bred.*
>
> Mahatma Gandhi [209]

SPREAD OF THE JAIN FAITH

Adapted from Ninian Smart, *Atlas of World Religions*, 53.[210]

ORIGIN OF INDIA'S THREE VEGETARIAN FAITHS

THE HINDU FAITH
THE BUDDHIST FAITH
THE JAIN FAITH

Adapted from Ninian Smart, *Atlas of World Religions*, 38.[211]

The earliest sages of the Hindu faith lived in northwestern India along the banks of the Indus River and in the mountains of Kashmir and Punjab. Gautama Buddha, the founder of Buddhism, was born in southern Nepal, just north of India. During most of his life, he lived and taught in eastern India along the banks of the Ganges River. Mahavira, the most recent of the Jain spiritual leaders lived and taught in eastern India, in the same region as did Gautama Buddha, along the banks of the Ganges River.

Part II

Sacred Teachings Leading to
The Vegetarian Philosophy of India

PART II
SACRED TEACHINGS LEADING TO
THE VEGETARIAN PHILOSOPHY OF INDIA

THE VEGETARIAN PHILOSOPHY OF INDIA

For countless centuries, billions of people upon the subcontinent of India have chosen to live as vegetarians. They have done so with sincere dedication and conviction. Their motivations have not been those of quests for personal gain. Rather, they have been quests to live without inflicting harm upon any weaker being. Because these individuals feel so committed to lives of nonviolence, it is quite simple for them to live vegetarian lifestyles. Most could never imagine any other lifestyle.

Values of nonviolence have been so deeply entrenched within the Hindu faith that most Hindus live and breathe these values without even thinking about them. The Hindu concept of nonviolence is an all encompassing one. It involves embodying nonviolence in thought, word and deed—at all times and in all situations. When a child of Hindu faith is growing up, its family is a living example of nonviolence for all of its life.

To one of vegetarian Hindu heritage, nonviolence has been so much a part of life that there is no need to search the ancient sacred scriptures to learn of its origins. Such an individual has lived witnessing nonviolence all around.

Yet for one seeking further insight into the Hindu philosophy of nonviolence, a study of the sacred Hindu scriptures is a key that unlocks the door to understanding this philosophy. For it has been the deeply meaningful and spiritually profound teachings of the ancient Hindu scriptures, teachings passed on orally from generation to generation, that set the ground-work for the vegetarian philosophy of India.

One seeking to understand the vegetarian philosophy of India will do well to start at its beginnings. For it has been from the most fundamental of Hinduism's spiritual and philo-sophical concepts that its teachings of nonviolence and vegetarianism arose.

Any inquiry into the vegetarian philosophy of India must also include an inquiry into the sacred scriptures of Buddhist and Jain faiths. Although only a small percent of present day Indians are of Buddhist or Jain faith, over the centuries, the supportive philosophies among India's three vegetarian faiths—Hinduism, Buddhism and the Jain faith—have contributed to the flourishing of each. This support ensured that the lands of India would become the soil upon which the philosophy of compassionate vegetarianism would take root and blossom.

The following analysis of religious-philosophical scriptural concepts will lead one to understand why it is that billions of people upon the subcontinent of India have chosen to lead nonharming, nonviolent, nonkilling, vegetarian lives. The analysis incorporates meaningful concepts from Hindu, Buddhist, and Jain scriptures. Because Hinduism is the most ancient, and the largest, of India's three vegetarian faiths, this analysis focuses upon it.

Within this cascade of sacred teachings, one concept leads to the next. Those teachings concerning the belief in God, however, are confined solely to the Hindu faith. Neither Buddhist nor Jain faiths involve the concept of a deity. Nevertheless, all three faiths involve *Laws of Karma* and *Laws of Rebirth*. Although many Hindu, Buddhist, and Jain teachings arrive at the same conclusion—the conclusion that one should show mercy, kindness, and compassion to all beings—each arrives there by following a different path. The following study begins with an explanation of the Hindu belief in God.

THE HINDU CONCEPT OF GOD

GOD EXISTS

Hinduism is a religion committed to the belief in God. To a Hindu, God is of such omnipotence and of such magnificence that God pervades all existence. God is manifest in all. God is distant, yet also near. God is within, and without. God resides within the greatest of transcendent phenomenon, and also within the smallest of microscopic beings. God is not merely confined to any one location. God is in all and God is all.

> *He is my Self within the heart, smaller than a grain of rice, smaller than a grain of barley, smaller than a mustard-seed, smaller than a canary seed or the kernel of a canary seed. He is my Self within the heart, greater than the earth, greater than the sky, greater than the heaven, greater than all these worlds.*
>
> *Chandogya Upanishad*[1]

To one of Hindu faith, God is so all encompassing and all pervading that the Soul of God is perceived as being present within all creation. It is the essence of God that gives all else meaning. The essence that resides within all that lives, breathes, and feels, is viewed as containing a portion of God. God's presence penetrates all that has ever existed, all that presently exists, and all that will ever exist.

The foundational concepts of Hinduism begin with the Hindu *Vedas*. Within each *Veda*, it is the *Upanishads* that contain a preponderance of the philosophical concepts. The *Upanishads* teach that all creation originates from, exists in, and returns to God. God is sometimes referred to as *Brahman*, God in the universe, and sometimes referred to as *Atman*, the Self of God. *Brahman* is both a tangible and a transcendent entity. *Atman* is the emotionally feeling Soul of all. The terms *Brahman* and *Atman* are concepts upon which the Hindu vision of God is based.[2]

God, or *Brahman,* is all encompassing. God is within all that has form and all that is form-less. God is the essence from which all emanates and that to which all will return. God is the unfathomable soul within all beings. The *Upanishads* describe God, *Brahman,* thus:

> *He is the refuge of all. In Him exists all that moves and breathes. Adorable is He. He is the supreme goal. He is beyond the known, and beyond the knowable. He is self-luminous, subtler than the sub-tlest; in Him exist all the worlds and all those that live therein. He is the imperishable Brahman.*
>
> *Upanishad*[3]

The level of omnipotence of God, as recognized within the Hindu faith, is described in the following passage.

> *Brahman shines by its own light. By its light all this universe is illuminated. The sun, moon, stars, fire and lightening shine by its light. No one can live and breathe if there were not the self-lumi-nous Brahman.*
>
> *Keno Upanishad*[4]

72

GOD IS ETERNAL

In Hinduism, God is perceived as an eternally and infinitely existing phenomenon. God has always existed, does exist, and will continue to exist—eternally.

Brahman is birthless, deathless, decayless, eternal, pure, unconditional, one without a second. It is the Self or Atman of all beings.
Keno Upanishad[5]

The universe is transitory, perishable, and changing. Brahman, on the contrary, is eternal, undecaying, and immutable.
Swami Nikhilananda[6]

ALL CREATION IS A MANIFESTATION OF GOD

In Hinduism, God is not perceived solely as a distant being, an aloof spirit, or a hidden wizard. Rather, God is perceived as that which has created all, moves all, and is within all. God is here and now. God can be found in the most humble of beggars and the most profound of thinkers. God is recognized as that essence that forms and sustains every single event in the cosmos. God is the substrate from which all in existence has been created. God is the energy by which every occurrence is set in motion.

> *The Lord of Love willed: "Let me be many!" And in the depths of his meditation, He created everything that exists.*
>
> *Taittiriya Upanishad*[7]

> *The Self (the Atman), the animated energy in all living beings, is the substratum or support of all beings.*
>
> *Isavasya Upanishad*[8]

Speaking as a manifestation of God, Krishna states in the *Bhagavad Gita*

> *I am the Soul dwelling in the heart of everything. I am the Beginning, the Middle, and the End. Of the lights I am the sun. Of the stars I am the moon. Of those that measure I am time. I am death that destroys all and I am the origin of things that are yet to be born. The germ of all living things is myself.*
>
> *Bhagavad Gita*[9]

GOD MANIFESTS IN INFINITE FORMS

One of Hindu faith sees God as present in all creation and in all creatures. He or she sees God in the sun and the moon, in the first drops of morning dew, and in the first cries of a newborn baby. God is ever present and shows Its presence in an infinite number of ways and an infinite number of forms.

> *He is the bluebird, he is the green bird with red eyes; he is the thundercloud, and he is the seasons and the seas . . . He is the source from which the worlds evolve.*
>
> *Shvetashvatara Upanishad*[10]

To a Hindu, God is not defined as one singular entity. God, though one in essence, manifests in a limitless number of forms and an infinite number of actions.

> *As many as are mentioned in "the hymn to the Vishvedevas," namely, three hundred and three, three thousand and three.*
>
> *Brihadaranyaka Upanishad*[11]

God Reveals to All Differently

Because God is present in all, God does not exist solely in the heavens. God is equally present on the land and in the seas. God does not mingle solely with the lofty, forsaking the lowly. God does not clamor for the great, shrinking from the meek. God is in all, pervades all, and can be found in all. One has but to search to find God in all. Accordingly, God can reveal from any location, within any object, from any being, and in any form. And, God can reveal differently to all people.

Krishna, in the *Bhagavad Gita*, as a human manifestation of God, tells Arjuna that because God is so powerful, God possesses the capabilities of presenting to all differently. In so doing, God helps all people and all beings perceive the divine in whatever form they will best be able to relate.

> *Those who worship other gods with faith and devotion also worship me.*
>
> *Bhagavad Gita*[12]

THEREFORE, ALL PERCEIVE GOD DIFFERENTLY

Knowing that God possesses the ability to present to all differently, one can understand how, or why, Hindus accept the religious beliefs of people of all faiths. Hindus embrace the concept that God presents to all differently and, therefore, respect the concept that all people of all faiths perceive God differently. Reflecting upon the many manifestations through which God presents within Hindu mythology in the *Puranas*, Radhakrishnan states

> *Hindu thought believes in the evolution of our knowledge of God.*
> *It accepts the obvious fact that humankind seeks its goal of God at*
> *various levels and in various directions, and feels sympathy with*
> *every stage of the search.*
>
> Radhakrishnan[13]

GOD CREATES, SUSTAINS AND RECLAIMS ALL

ALL LIFE IS BORN OF GOD

One of Hindu faith believes that God creates all in existence from Its own being.

In the beginning was only Being . . . Out of Himself He brought forth the cosmos and entered into everything. There is nothing that does not come from Him.

Chandogya Upanishad[14]

The Great Lord is the beginning, the cause that unites [the soul with the body].

Svetasvatara Upanishad[15]

As a spider moves along the thread [that it produces], and as from a fire tiny sparks fly in all directions, so from the Self emanate all organs and all the worlds, all gods, and all beings.

Brihadaranyaka Upanishad[16]

Within Hindu philosophy, not only does God create all life, but God also remains within all life. *Brahman,* God, creates, preserves, and destroys all creation through a cyclic course of birthing, sustaining, and retaking. Then, God recommences the cycle—perpetually.

> *One the all-pervading sun; One the Dawn, spreading her light over the earth. All that exists is one, whence is produced the whole world.*
>
> Ṛg Veda[17]

Such ancient teachings, as the *Ṛg Veda,* express the Hindu concept that all creation is unified in one cyclic, perpetual flow. Though the life of each aspect of creation may seem fleeting, the essence of each is united with all others and is eternal. The sun produces the dawn, the dawn spreads over the earth and the earth comes alive. The sun's rays, however, are not gone. They exist amidst the new life they have helped to form upon the earth.

Creating, sustaining, and taking life are envisioned as one continuous flow. It is through God's unseen laws of physics that creation's cycles of existence are born. These include cycles such as day following night, high tide following low tide, and summer following winter. Although some aspects of creation may seem unchanged, this is just a perception. God sustains all for whatever time God has allotted to each. Yet each is just lying dormant, awaiting God's call to recycle within God's perpetual cycle of existence.

To a Hindu, God is the only aspect of creation that is permanent. The outer shell of any being decays and passes away. Yet God sustains that being's soul. In Hindu philosophy, each soul is part of the perpetual Soul of God.

> *The Self [God] is the sun shining in the sky, the wind blowing in space: He is the fire at the altar and in the home (of) the guest; He dwells in human beings, in gods, in truth, and in the vast firmament.*
>
> Katho Upanishad[18]

ALL LIFE MUST RETURN TO GOD

Hindu scriptures teach that it is the destiny of all creation to unite with God, *Brahman*.

> *That from which these beings are born, that in which when born*
> *they live, and that into which they enter at their death is Brahman.*
> *Taittiriya Upanishad*[19]

The *Upanishads* teach that those whose hearts are full of love will attain realization of God. Such individuals recognize that just as they emanate from God, so too, they must return.

> *Imperishable is the Lord of Love. As from a blazing fire thousands*
> *of sparks leap forth, so millions of beings arise from the Lord of*
> *Love and return to him.*
> *Mundaka Upanishad*[20]

In Hindu teachings, when one lives a life of pure humble kindness, one's soul eliminates all accumulated negative energy. This soul, after having fulfilled its physical cycle, will return to the pure energy of God.

> *He creates all the worlds, and maintains and finally withdraws them*
> *into Himself.*
> *Svetasvatara Upanishad*[21]

God is In All

The *Upanishads* teach that God is in all creation, and therefore, all creation is God. Because all beings emanate from God's Universal Self, all beings are a part of God. When one can perceive the Self of God in all, one will see God's presence in every being and in everything—everywhere. One will also sense the essence of God within oneself, and will attain inner peace.

> *This Self is all in all. He is all the gods, the five elements, earth, air, fire, water, and space; all creatures great or small, born of eggs, of heat, of shoots; all horses, cows, elephants, men, and women; all beings that walk, all beings that fly, and all that neither walk nor fly.*
>
> Aitareya Upanishad[22]

The *Bhagavad Gita* expresses the Hindu concept that God lives within all beings.

> *My true being is unborn and changeless. I am the Lord who dwells in every creature.*
>
> Bhagavad Gita[23]

God is in the Heart of Every Creature

The *Isha Upanishad* is often presented as the first *Upanishad*. It expresses some of the most fundamental concepts of Hinduism. Mahatma Gandhi has said that if all other Hindu texts were to disappear, the initial passages of the *Isha Upanishad* would still embody the teachings of the Hindu faith.

> *The Lord is enshrined in the hearts of all . . . All belongs to the Lord.*
>
> *Isha Upanishad*[24]

To one of Hindu faith, God is perceived as being present within the hearts of all. It is considered the destiny of all to return to God.

> *There is one Ruler who rules all the world by His powers. There is no one besides Him who can make Him the second. He is present inside the hearts of all beings.*
>
> *Shvetashvatara Upanishad*[25]

> *Even as the sun shines and fills all space with light, above, below, across, so shines the Lord of Love and fills the hearts of all created beings.*
>
> *Shvetashvatara Upanishad*[26]

> *Hidden in the heart of every creature exists the Self, subtler than the subtlest, greater than the greatest.*
>
> *Katha Upanishad*[27]

> *God, the Maker of All, is ever seated in the heart of all creatures.*
>
> *Svetasvatara Upanishad*[28]

The concept of a soul, or an inner self, originated in early Vedic times. The soul is not perceived as being bound within the physical confines of the body. Rather, when the physical body dies, the soul lives on passing from being to being. The first time the soul is mentioned is in the *Shatapatha Brahmana*. This concept is developed further in the *Upanishads*, the *Laws of Manu*, and the *Puranas*.

In Hinduism, a term oftentimes used to describe the Soul of God is the *atman*. A portion of the Soul, or Self, of God resides within each being. This portion of the soul of God within each being is generally termed an *atman*. The *atman* continues to exist within a series of beings in a cyclic continuum of existences. During this recycling, the *atman* experiences repeated births, deaths, and rebirths in various life forms.[29] The Soul of God exists eternally in all.

> *As the web issues out of the spider and . . . as hair grows from the body, even so . . . the universe springs from the deathless Self, the source of life.*
>
> *Mundaka Upanishad*[30]

Hence, no form of existence is distinct from any other form, and no time in the spectrum of eternity is distinct, unrelated, or separate from any other time. Rather, all forms and all eras are of one continuous essence. The Universal Self of God is, always has been, and always will be, the same Self in all—eternally.

> *That which is invisible, ungraspable, without family, without cast. Eternal, all-pervading, omnipresent, exceedingly subtle; that is the Imperishable.*
>
> *Mundaka Upanishad*[31]

As the philosophy of Hinduism evolved, God became recognized as having an eternal Self.

> *The Self is the sun shining in the sky, the wind blowing in space. . . .*
> *He is in human beings, in gods, in truth. And in the vast firmament:*
> *He is the fish born of water, the plant growing in the earth, the river*
> *flowing down from the mountain. For this Self is supreme!*
> *Katha Upanishad*[32]

The Self of God is recognized as residing not just in other beings, but also in oneself. As explained through a series of deductions in the A*itareya, Brihadaranyaka, Chandogya,* and *Mundaka Upanishads,*

> *At first there was the Atman alone.*
> *All this is Atman.*
> *There was only Being at the beginning, it was one without a second.*
> *All this is Brahman.*
> *This self is the Brahman.*
> *I am Brahman.*[33]

Through such teachings, one of Hindu faith learns to realize that all beings, including one's own self, possess a portion of the *"Atman,"* the Soul of God.

GOD IS THE INDWELLING SPIRIT OF ALL CREATION

God pervades all in existence. God also pervades all not in existence. Although few can perceive God's eternal presence, God is the source of all matter and energy. God is the initial force, the driving energy, and the spirit that sustains all existence—perpetually.

> *There abides forever in the unborn in the secret place within the body. He moves through the earth but the earth knows him not . . . He alone is the indwelling spirit of all beings.*
>   *Shvetashvatara Upanishad*[34]

The *Upanishads* teach that all beings possess an essence of the *Atman*, the Soul of God, within them. As the soul of each being is a fragment of the Soul of God, all beings are One within God's Soul.

> *The soul of an ant is the same as the soul of an elephant. There is*
> *one Common Consciousness in all beings.*
> *Katho Upanishad*[35]

People often mistakenly identify themselves solely by their bodies. But these are merely the external sheaths they have been given to transport their souls. They feel pride of ownership in their own shell, and do not relate to the needs of other beings. Hinduism teaches that all creation is derived from the same energy source and that all in creation possess the same longings and emotions. Each being is not separate from any other being. One might wonder why all appear different. The Hindu scriptures explain such differences through metaphors, e.g.: Just as fire, being one in its essence, assumes different forms according to that which is being burned, the *Brahman* assumes different forms according to what it enters.[36]

Hinduism teaches that one's consciousness is not an isolated entity. It does not suddenly come into existence and it is never destroyed. In the *Brihadaranyaka Upanishad*, King Janaka asks the sage, Yajnavalkya, "What serves a man for a light?" Yajnavalkya responds that it the sun. He goes on to answer a series of Janaka's questions by answering that when the sun goes down, it is the moon; and when the moon has set, it is the fire; and when the fire goes out, it is the voice; and when the voice is silenced, it is the essence of God that serves as the source of light for all.

> *The Self serves as his light. It is through the light of the Self that he*
> *sits, goes out, works, and returns home.*
> *Brihadaranyaka Upanishad*[37]

The Self is the infinite Consciousness dwelling within each being. It is that which remains after every trace of individuality is removed. It is pure being. The sages called it *Brahman* from the root *brih*, to expand.[38] It is not merely one's intellect. It is the irreducible ground for existence. It is the light within each and every being's heart.

> *The Self is the common consciousness of all beings.*
> *Isavasya Upanishad*[39]

God Pervades Everywhere and Everything

God Pervades All that is Seen

Hindu philosophy teaches that God is present in the grandeur of all creation and in the minuteness of each tiny aspect of it. God is in the great and the modest. God is everywhere and nowhere.

> *God is not some person outside ourselves or away from the universe.*
> *He pervades everything, and is omniscient as well as omnipotent.*
> Mahatma Gandhi
> Ashram Observances in Action (1959)[40]

> *He is the fish born in water, the plant growing in the earth, The*
> *river flowing down from the mountain. He is the self-supreme!*
> *Katho Upanishad[41]*

GOD PERVADES ALL THAT IS UNSEEN

The *Upanishads* teach that God pervades, sustains, and unites all creation as one—all that can be seen and all that is beyond seeing. Though the human being cannot perceive that which is beyond his or her five senses, the energy of God pervades everywhere and everything. God's essence is far beyond humankind's limited senses. God's presence pervades the invisible, the microscopic, and the transcendent—God's presence pervades all that is beyond knowing.

> *The Lord of Love is above name and form. He is present in all and*
> *transcends all. . . . From him comes every body and mind. He is the*
> *source of space, air, fire, water, and the earth that holds us all.*
> *Mundaka Upanishad* [42]

God is present in stillness and in motion, and in the tangible and the transcendent.

> *It is resting and yet restless, it is far and still so near! It is inside all*
> *and still outside all.*
> *Isha Upanishad*[43]

The *Puranas* tell that God dwells in all creation and in all creatures, oftentimes in subtle forms too small for the human eye to see, termed *Jivatma*. Though unseen, God is ever present.

> *In all the Beings and things of the world, inclusive of worms, flies,*
> *trees and grasses, remains the Lord unseen by the naked eye.*
> *Bhagavata Purana*[44]

ALL CREATION IS ONE

ALL CREATION IS GOD

In Hinduism, all creation is perceived as a manifestation of God. Actually, there is nothing else but God. Though differing in form, nothing would exist were it not for the unseen power of God. The *Upanishads* assist one to recognize God as the force that moves all and as the love compelling all.

Heavenly is the spirit, the formless one; It is outside and inside, the unborn one, devoid of breath, devoid of desire, the pure one . . . . Out of it originates the breath, the mind and all the senses, out of it arises ether, wind, and fire and the waters and the earth which bears everything.

Mundaka Upanishad[45]

The ancient ageless one, omnipresent in all, penetrating all, as self in all with his origin denied. Those who have knowledge of the Brahman, name him as the eternal one.

Shvetashvatara Upanishad[46]

Recognizing that God is present within each and every facet of creation, a Hindu perceives all apparent diversity as an illusion. All are just varying manifestations of God.

> *The supreme Soul is identical with the individual and with all creation.*
>
> *Katha Upanishad*[47]

The Hindu Philosophy of Vedanta of Sankara teaches that one's existence is just a fleeting moment within the infinite and continuous cycle of creation. All beings and all existence must accept their humble roles within God's timeless flow of past, present, and future. All creation is part of God.[48]

> *The existence of Brahman . . . [is the]. . . Self of every one.*[49]

An understanding of the Hindu *Law of Karma* and *Law of Rebirth* serves to increase one's understanding of these concepts. The *Laws* teach that although one's physical body lasts but a fleeting moment, one's soul passes on to other beings, like changing garments, lasting eternally. The soul, however, cannot recall its past. Nor can it envision its future. That is because it passes through its series of lives encased in a different body during each existence. The soul, under normal circumstances, does not remember the events surrounding any of its prior existences.

The life of each being, while used as a shell to carry the soul, follows a course determined by the actions of that soul in its prior lives. Similarly, the actions of that soul during its present life will determine the difficulties and joys that soul must endure in its future lives.[50] All life is a continuum in which past and present actions redirect future events. Within this continuum, the actions of each and every being are of tremendous importance to all in existence—eternally.

There is one all-pervading Atman (Self). It is the innermost soul of all beings. If you injure your neighbor, you really injure yourself. If you injure any other creature, you really injure yourself, because the whole world is really nothing but yourself.

Swami Sivananda[51]

The *Upanishads* teach that God is present within all that ever was and all that ever will be. God exists in perpetuity and it is God's tiny spark that rests in the heart of every being.

The Lord of Love is hidden in the heart of every creature, subtler than the subtlest, greater than the greatest.

Shvetashvatara Upanishad[52]

Everything in the cosmos—energy and space, fire and water, name and form . . . all come from the Self. The Self is one, though it appears to be many.

Chandogya Upanishad[53]

The *Upanishads* tell of the Absolute Unity of all in existence. This Absolute Unity encompasses the Soul of God, the entire universe, and the souls of all beings. God is present in all things, within them and without, seen and unseen. The Soul of God is present within the soul of each and every being. God is the past, present, and future. All that can be conceived, imagined, or dreamed of is, essentially, the Soul of God.

The sage sees all beings in the Self and the Self in all beings. The sage who has realized the Self beholds that all objects and all beings are not distinct from his own Self, and that his Self is the same Self in all.

Isavasya Upanishad[54]

Each Aspect of Creation is One with All Others

The *Upanishads* describe life as one unit in which all aspects of creation vibrate in harmony with all other aspects. Hindu sages recognized that an aura of energy radiates from all matter. Each aura radiates concentrically from its source and influences all other auras around it. By affecting all other auras, the energy of each being affects the course of all other energy fields, now and throughout infinity.

Recognizing this, spiritually advanced Hindus strive to show mercy and respect toward all other beings—human, non-human, and even invisible. They distribute food to birds, animals, and fish before they even consider eating themselves. They realize the enormous potential each and every being possesses in spreading positive energy. They see a portion of the Self of God within the self of each being.

> *The Self is the same in the king and the peasant, the saint and the sinner, the cobbler and the barber, the ant and the elephant, the tree and the stone.*
>
> *Isavasya Upanishad*[55]

Recognizing that matter and energy are just variations in form within the continuing cycle of existence, a Hindu feels a bond with all other aspects of creation.

> *Thou art woman. Thou art man. Thou art the youth and the maiden too. Thou art an old man totterest with a staff.*
>
> *Shvetashvatara Upanishad*[56]

> *He who recognizes all beings here in his own self and himself in all that lives—he never feels alarmed before any one.*
>
> *Isha Upanishad*[57]

> *Being born, thou becomest facing in every direction. . . . Thou art the seasons and the seas. Having no beginning, thou dost abide with immanence, wherefore all beings are born.*
>
> *Shvetashvatara Upanishad*[58]

Perceiving all creation as a manifestation of God, one of Hindu faith feels a sense of concern and devotion for the essence of God within each aspect of creation.[59] Through such devotion toward all God's creation, a Hindu attains a sense of union with the divine.

> *Through unfailing devotion, Arjuna, you can know me, see me, and attain union with me.*
>
> *Bhagavad Gita*[60]

The *Puranas* guide one to live a virtuous life. These include their teaching values of dispassion and detachment, sacrifice of possesions, moderation and abstinence, and the cultivation of inner tranquility.[61]

> *Vishnu is most pleased with him who does good to others, who neither beats nor slays any living thing, who is ever diligent in the service of the gods and of brahmins and his teachers, who always desires the welfare of all creatures, as of his children and of his own soul.*
>
> *Vishnu Purana III*[62]

The *Upanishads* reinforce this concept, teaching that each aspect of creation is a manifestation of God, and each aspect should be loved for the essence of God within it.[63]

> *Creatures are loved not for their own sake, but because the Self lives in them. Everything is loved not for its own sake, but because the Self lives in it.*
>
> *Brihadaranyaka Upanishad*[64]

Hindu, Buddhist and Jain Laws of Karma and Rebirth

The Law of Karma

According to the *Law of Karma*, the totality of one's thoughts, words, and deeds, the sum of all one's actions, in one's present and prior lifetimes, affect one's soul in future existences. Although one is not able to trace, consciously, a direct path from one's past to one's future, all will be accounted for!

> *As the night follows day, evil that we do recoils on us.*
>
> *Tirukkural*[65]

Hindu philosophy teaches that if one follows a life of total selflessness, one can wipe out one's prior negative *karma*, and return to the pure energy of God.

> *Those who practice austerity and faith in the forest, the tranquil knowers who live the life of a mendicant, depart free from sin, through the door of the sun to where dwells the immortal, imperishable person.*
>
> *Mundaka Upanishad*[66]

Hinduism's *Law of Karma* teaches that as a person thinks, speaks, and acts, so he or she becomes.

> *As a person acts, so he becomes in life. Those who do good become good; Those who do harm become bad. So we are said to be what our desire is. As our desire is, so is our will. As our will is, so are our acts. As we act, so we become.*
>
> *Brihadaranyaka Upanishad*[67]

The *Yoga Sutras* teach that the only pure works are those derived from those seeking *ahimsa* as their primary goal:

> *Therefore let everyone first examine well and then utter truth for the benefit of all living beings.*
>
> *Surendranath Dasgupta*[68]

Pantanjali, the ancient Hindu sage of the *Yoga Sutras*, guided followers away from superficial and impure thoughts. He felt that even the thought of violence would create an endless trail of negative *karma*.

> *As improper thoughts, emotions (and actions), such as those of violence, etc., whether they are done (indulged in), caused to be done or abetted, whether present in mild, medium, or intense degree, result in endless pain and ignorance.*
>
> *Yoga Sutra*[69]

The *Laws of Karma* in Hindu, Buddhist, and Jain philosophies, though based upon different foundational concepts, believe that any thought or act that contributes to violence leaves a trail of negative *karma*.

> *All suffering befalls those who inflict harm on others. Those who desire immunity from suffering never commit injury.*
>
> *Tirukkural*[70]

Similarly, Buddhist Sacred writings state that

> *He who, seeking his own happiness, punishes or kills beings who also long for happiness, will not find happiness after death.*
>
> *Dhammapada*[71]

THE LAW OF REBIRTH

The *Upanishads* teach that the Soul of God is the same soul within each and every being. The soul exists in perpetuity within a perpetual cycle of rebirths—eternally throughout all time and all space.

> *All these creatures also know not, though they have come forth*
> *again out of the Being . . . whether they may be here a tiger or a*
> *lion or a wolf or a boar or a worm or a bird or a gadfly or a gnat,*
> *whatever they may be, they are again born.*
>
> *Chandogya Upanishad*[72]

Yet one who lives a life of total selfless love can obtain release from the cycle of rebirth and return to the peace of the Great Unknown.

> *On this ever-revolving wheel of being, the individual self goes round*
> *and round through life after life, believing itself to be a separate*
> *creature, until it sees its identity with the Love of the Lord.*
>
> *Shvetashvatara Upanishad*[73]

The *Law of Karma* and *Law of Rebirth*, when combined, teach that throughout the ever-turning cycle of birth, life, and death, each and every action affects all creation—infinitely. Each and every action, each and every word, and each and every thought produce an eternal trail of *karma*.

> *As many hairs as the slain beast has, so often indeed will he who*
> *killed it without a (lawful) reason suffer a violent death in future*
> *births.*
>
> *Laws of Manu*[74]

The results of one's actions may not be immediately recognized, for the resultant effects span eternity.

> *The Self is born again and again in new bodies to work out the karma in future lives. The embodied self assumes many forms, heavy or light according to its needs for growth and for the deeds of previous lives. This evolution is a divine law.*
>
> *Shvetashvatara Upanishad*[75]

Hindu and Buddhist visions of the *Law of Rebirth* teach that all existence is entwined within a cyclic continuum of creation and re-creation. Within this continuum, even the tiniest act of compassion benefits all—perpetually.

> *He who seeking his own happiness does not punish or kill beings who also long for happiness, will find happiness after death.*
>
> *Dhammapada*[76]

In the Jain faith, the soul is viewed as passing through a series of continuous rebirths, the quality of each being determined by one's thoughts and actions in one's present and prior lives.[77] Jains also believe that one may be reborn into nonhuman realms, including the realm of submicroscopic life. Based upon this belief, a Jain places the responsibility for one's fate in one's own hands, not in the hands of a god.

Jains view each soul as being bound within its own cycle. Anyone who feels superior to any other being is misguided. Any being presently trapped within a specific life form may have been one's mother or father in a previous lifetime. Hence, Jains feel respect, compassion and kinship with all beings. Jains believe that each individual possesses the potential to live a perfect life, and each should strive to do so.

Jains view life at every level as meaningful—even insects in dung, organisms in water, and bacteria in fluids. They respect the life of even the humblest of beings

> *Born of the egg, born of the womb, born of dung, born of liquids –these are classes of living beings. Know that they all seek happiness. In hurting them men hurt themselves, and will be born again among them.*
>
> Sutrakṛtanga[78]

In the Jain faith, only a human has sufficient reasoning power to free oneself from the cycle of rebirths. To do so, one must perform all actions at the highest level of virtue. Only then will one avoid incurring karmic repercussions.

> *The same cruelty he has done in a former birth, the same will be inflicted on him in a Circle of Births. Having been [re]born in an extremely miserable state of life, the sufferer experiences infinite pain.*
>
> Sutrakṛtanga[79]

COMBINING HINDU CONCEPTS OF GOD, KARMA AND REBIRTH

ONE PERCEIVES ALL CREATION AS ONE FLOWING RIVER

Hindu scriptures teach that as surely as water from a tiny stream will someday return to the great ocean, the soul of all beings will someday return to the Soul of God.

> *Just as these rivers flowing towards the sea, when they have reached the sea disappear, their names and forms perish. All are called the sea (the enlightened soul) and become without parts and immortal.*
> *Prasna Upanishad*[80]

To a Hindu, though all creation ebbs and flows along its course, all inevitably unite with God's Universal Soul. Ancient sacred Hindu writings teach that an underlying energy, *prana*, sustains all beings, all evolution, and all time and space. Though the myriad aspects of creation may outwardly appear different, all are part of the one great flow of God. As small rivers lose their individual names when they reach the sea, so too, does each aspect of creation lose its earthly nature when it realizes the Soul of God.[81]

> *These rivers, my dear, flow, the eastern to the east; the western toward the west. They go just from the ocean to the ocean. They become the ocean itself. And there they know not "I am this one," "I am that one." Even so, indeed, my dear, all creatures here, though they have come forth from Being, know not "We have come forth from Being."*
> *Chandogya Upanishad*[82]

Similar concepts are echoed within the Hindu epic, the *Mahabharata*. Arjuna is taught that all in creation must end. Eventually and inevitably, all creation merges into the oneness of God:

> *Arjuna, in the Cauldron of Time we are all melted away until we lose ourselves. It is now time we melt and lose our individuality.*

> *Mahabharata*[83]

One who accepts that he or she is just a humble drop in creation's eternal flow will release all pride concerning one's present existence. Only then will one attain spiritual fulfillment.

> *Just as the rivers flow and disappear in the sea, giving up their name and form, so also, the wise man, released from name and form, enters into the divine highest spirit.*
> *Mundaka Upanishad*[84]

ONE PERCEIVES ALL CREATION AS A MANIFESTATION OF GOD

Hindu philosophy teaches that all in the universe was created in, arose in, and remains in God. And it is to God that all in the universe will return. It is this one God, amidst the multitude of all of Its creations, that the Hindu worships. Accordingly, Hindus have deep reverence for the practice of nonviolence, *ahimsa,* toward all—for they realize that all creatures and all creation are part of the cyclic essence of God.[85]

> *They see the Self in every creature and all creation in the Self. I am ever present to those who have realized me in every creature. Seeing all life as my manifestation, they are never separated from me.*
>
> *Bhagavad Gita*[86]

As one abandons one's ego, one will feel part of the infinite flow of energy of the universe. One will feel unity, concern, and oneness with all creation.

> *Where there is seperateness, one sees another, smells another, tastes another, speaks to another . . . . But where there is unity, one without a second, that is the world of Brahman.*
>
> *Brihadaranyaka Upanishad*[87]

Such an individual will recognize that beyond any superficial differences in form, all creation possesses an essence of God.

> *As oil in the oil seed (sesame), as the butter in milk, as water in the stream, as fire in the fuel stick—he finds in his own self that one (Atman).*
>
> *Svetasvatara Upanishad*[88]

Those who see the essence of God in every being, attain peace.

> *Those who enter the Self enter into the peace that brings complete self-control and perfect patience. They see themselves in everyone and everyone in themselves.*
>
> *Brihadaranyaka Upanishad*[89]

ONE PERCEIVES THE ESSENCE OF GOD WITHIN EACH BEING

The *Upanishads* teach one to recognize that because the Self of God has formed all, God is present in all. In one's humble, human state of consciousness, one must look past differences in external form and realize the presence of God in each.

> *See the Self in all, and go beyond death . . . the light of Brahman*
> *flashes in lightening . . . . He is the inmost Self of everyone; He*
> *alone is worthy of our love.*
> Keno Upanishad[90]

The *Svetashvatara Upanishad* teaches that it is God's Soul that is manifesting in the soul within each being. This soul exists in perpetuity amidst an eternal cycle of rebirths, manifesting in the hearts of all.

> *On this ever-revolving wheel of being, the individual self goes round*
> *and round through life after life, believing itself to be a separate*
> *creature, until it sees its identity with the Love of the Lord.*
> Shvetashvatara Upanishad[91]

> *He alone sees truly who sees the Lord in every creature.*
> Bhagavad Gita[92]

One Feels Equal concern for All Beings

Recognizing the Soul of God in all beings, one of Hindu faith does not fear other beings.

> *The Self seems to move, but is ever still. He seems far away, but is ever near. He is within all, and he transcends all. Those who see all creatures in themselves and themselves in all creatures know no fear.*
>
> *Isha Upanishad*[93]

> *When one realizes the Self . . . all life is one, changeless, nameless, formless, then one fears no more.*
>
> *Taittiriya Upanishad*[94]

Having attained such realization, one feels kinship will all beings.

> *From water and the moon, divine breath (spirit) enters into him. And verily that is divine breath which, whether moving or not moving, does not tire, and therefore does not perish. He who knows this, becomes the Self of all beings.*
>
> *Brihadaranyaka Upanishad*[95]

> *He who recognizes all beings here in his own self and himself in all that lives—he never feels alarmed before anyone.*
>
> *Isha Upanishad*[96]

Nothing moves him to love or hate, who finds all beings in himself and himself in all beings. What can delusion or sorrow mean then? When to the knower realizing unity in the All, every particle has become his Self.

Isha Upanishad[97]

In addition, those who see the Self of God in all creation recognize God's presence in themselves.

The intellect cannot reveal the Self, beyond its duality of subject and object. They who see themselves in all and all in them help others through spiritual osmosis to realize the Self themselves.

Katha Upanishad[98]

Based upon the ancient *Upanishad* teachings that the Soul of God is present in all creation, the *Bhagavad Gita* advises followers thus

They live in wisdom who see themselves in all and all in them.

Bhagavad Gita[99]

I look upon all creatures equally; none are less dear . . . and none more dear.

Bhagavad Gita[100]

The men of self-realization look with an equal eye on a Brahmin possessed of learning and humility, a cow, an elephant, a dog.

Bhagavad Gita[101]

The *Bhagavad Gita* teaches that through selfless action, one will identify with the whole of life; through giving, one will lose the concept of being an isolated self; through devotion, one will find God.

> *The infinite joy of touching Brahman [God] is easily attained by those who are free from the burden of evil and established within themselves. They see the Self in every creature and all creation in the Self.*
>
> *Bhagavad Gita*[102]

> *United with Brahman, ever joyful, beyond the reach of desire and sorrow, he has equal regard for every living creature and attains full devotion to me.*
>
> *Bhagavad Gita*[103]

ONE SEEKS TO PROTECT ALL BEINGS

Passages of the *Atharva Veda* reveal that even during Hinduism's formative years, many had been practicing deeply meditative yogic practices to reach higher levels of consciousness. Having attained these, they were able to feel a unity with all creation. Hence, they sought to protect all beings and even sought to aid lower life forms in attaining spiritual fulfillment.

> *Those noble souls who practice meditation and other yogic ways, who are ever careful about all beings, who protect all animals, they also care for our spiritual progress. They always take care that our behavior does not afflict any animal.*
> *Atharva Veda*[104]

Such teachings fostered the belief that the blessings of a peaceful life should be shared with all beings.

> *Righteousness was declared for restraining creatures from injuring one another. Therefore, that is righteous which prevents injury to creatures.*
> *Mahabharata*[105]

One Feels Compassion for All Beings

The concept of compassion for all beings permeates the entirety of Hindu philosophy. It includes not killing any being, not harming any being, and not causing any being to suffer grief. Hinduism's aversion to harming or taking the life of another being has led to a sense of compassion for all beings.

He who sees himself in all beings and all beings in himself, he goes thereby, and in no other way, into the abode of the highest Brahman.

Kaivalya Upanishad[106]

Let all be happy; let all enjoy perfect health; let all find the good of their heart; let none come to grief.

Kaivalya Upanishad[107]

Do not get angry or harm any living creature. Be compassionate and gentle. Show good will to all.

Bhagavad Gita[108]

The compassion as described within the *Upanishads* is not limited to one life form or to one circumstance. As expressed within the *Isha Upanishad*

> *A man endowed with Self-Knowledge remains undisturbed by the outer manifestations of ugliness or beauty, strength or weakness, saintliness or sinfulness; he feels love and compassion for all and for the welfare of all.*
>
> *Isha Upanishad*[109]

With such wisdom, one recognizes that

> *Life is as dear to all beings as it is to oneself; feel compassion for every being taking thy own Self as the measure.*
>
> *Brihadaranyaka Upanishad*[110]

Harboring such beliefs, one will look upon all beings as friends:

> *May all beings behold me with the eye of a friend. I behold all beings with the eyes of a friend. We behold each other with the eyes of a friend.*
>
> *Vajasanehi Samhita*[111]

One only hopes that he or she shows kindness toward all.

> *May I be dear to all animals.*
>
> *Atharva Veda*[112]

109

COMBINING THE WISDOM OF HINDU, BUDDHIST & JAIN FAITHS

THE PHILOSOPHY OF NONVIOLENCE (*AHIMSA*)

It is because of the cumulative wisdom contained within the sacred teachings of India's three vegetarian faiths, the Hindu, Buddhist, and Jain faiths, that the philosophy of non-violence permeates the entire subcontinent of India. The following passages exemplify the essence of their spiritual teachings.

It is the supremest virtue not to commit at any time even slight injury to others.

Tirukkural[113]

He who does not seek to cause the sufferings of bondage and death to living creatures, (but) desires the good of all (beings), attains endless bliss.

Laws of Manu[114]

All the scriptures emphasize the virtue of hospitality and the creed of non-violence.

Tirukkural[115]

That mode of living which is founded upon total harmlessness towards all creatures or (in case of actual necessity) upon a minimum of such harm, is the highest morality.

Mahabharata[116]

He who does not injure any (creature), attains without an effort what he thinks of, and what he undertakes, and what he fixes his mind on.

Laws of Manu[117]

Abstention from injury, by act, thought, and word, in respect of all creatures . . . constitutes behavior that is worthy of praise.

Mahabharata[118]

When there is natural firmness in non-violence all hostility comes to an end in its very presence.

Yoga Sutra[119]

In the *Mahabharata*, Yudhishthira, feeling love for all beings, cannot bear to harm any creature. He is ready to sacrifice his life for that of his dog.

My lord, you are asking me to do something, which I cannot do. This dog has shared all my troubles so far. It has been devoted to me. I cannot abandon this dog . . . . All the acts of mine, which have earned this heaven for me, will be destroyed if I behave without compassion towards this dog.

Mahabharata[120]

The *Upanishads* guide one to consider all beings as equals, and to seek peace and non-injury for all.

> *In so far as he gives shelter to all men, he becomes the world of men. In so far as he gives grass and water to the animals, he becomes the world of animals. In so far as beasts and birds, even to the ants, find a living in his house, he becomes their world . . . Verily as one wishes non-injury for his own world, so all beings wish non-injury.*
> Brihadaranyaka Upanishad[121]

The *Yoga Sutras* advise one to cultivate compassion towards any and all beings suffering pain, and to feel no ill will toward any of them. Only when practicing total *ahimsa* in mind, speech, and action, will one elevate oneself to higher levels of consciousness.[122]

> *[Ahimsa is] a great universal duty which a man should impose on himself in all conditions of life, everywhere, and at all times without restricting or qualifying it with any limitations whatsoever.*
> *Yoga Sutras*[123]

Nonviolence can be recognized at its highest level of commitment within the ascetic communities of the Jain faith.

> *The ascetic rejects the act of killing any life-forms whatsoever. [The Ascetic seeks to] avoid violence, whether performing it himself, compelling another to perform it, or approving another carrying it out, mentally, vocally and physically. In living according to this vow, the ascetic must closely observe where he walks so as to avoid stepping on and injuring any life forms in any way.*
> First Vow of a Jain Ascetic[124]

Through teachings of these Hindu, Buddhist and Jain sacred scriptures, values of nonviolence emerged, evolved, and disseminated throughout the vast lands of India.

By non-violence, one attains the supreme state.

Laws of Manu[125]

Teachings of the *Tirukkural* were incorporated into the Basavanna movement, 1131 to 1167 CE, and contributed to religious and social reform throughout India. They also became the moral foundation of the Virashaiva movement.

As all infinite beings bear the essence of the Divine in them, do not hurt them. If you hurt them it is as bad as hurting God Himself.[126]

THE PHILOSOPHY OF NONKILLING

Sacred scripture of India's three vegetarian faiths contain numerous passages, teachings, and pleadings for compassion, nonviolence, and nonkilling of all beings. These teachings can be traced to one of India's most ancient writings, the *Samhita* of the *Yajur Veda*

> *You must not use your God-given body for killing God's creatures,*
> *whether they are human, animal, or what ever they are.*
>   *Yajur Veda Samhita*[127]

Such teachings have been perpetuated within the *Tirukkural*

> *The whole world folds its hands in prayer to one who kills not and*
> *abjures flesh.*
>   *Tirukkural*[128]

And the *Laws of Manu*

> *By not killing any living being, one becomes fit for salvation.*
>   *Laws of Manu*[129]

They have also been reinforced by the Buddhist scriptures, wherein sadness over the slaying of cattle for sacrifice is expressed.

> *Not with their feet, nor with their horns do the cows hurt (anyone in*
> *any way and) yielding vessels (of milk)—(still) seizing them by the*
> *horns the kings cause them to be slain with a weapon.*
>   *Brahmanadhammikasutta*[130]

The *Bhagavata Purana* advises one never to kill any helpless being.

> *All creatures of entire creation from monkey to mosquito, bird, camel, deer, mouse, snakes, and insects too, treat them as offspring one and all. The soul in them being the same reflection of the Supreme Soul as in man. Harass them not in deed, word and mind, never.*
>
> *Bhagavata Purana*[131]

Buddhist scriptures send forth a plea that no one take the life of any being for any reason.

> *[One living a holy life] Let him not kill, nor cause to be killed any living being, nor let him approve of others killing.*
>
> *Dhammikasutta*[132]

Emperor Asoka sought to spread values of nonviolence and nonkilling by teaching the people moral prescriptions and meditation.

> *The people can be induced to advance in Dharma by only two means, by moral prescriptions and by meditation. . . . The moral prescriptions I have promulgated include rules making certain animals inviolable, and many others. But even in the case of abstention from injury and from killing living creatures, it is by meditation that people have progressed in Dharma most.*
>
> *Asoka's Pillar Edict VII*[133]

Values of nonviolence and nonkilling have been fostered by Jain teachings. In these teachings, acts of violence are recognized as the cause of a cycle of repercussions.

> *If a man kills living beings, or causes other men to kill them, or consents to the killing of them, his iniquity will go on increasing.*
>
> *Jain Sutrakritanga*[134]

> *This is the quintessence of wisdom: not to kill anything.*
>
> *Jain Sutrakritanga*[135]

THE RECOGNITION THAT MEAT CANNOT BE OBTAINED
WITHOUT INFLICTING SUFFERING AND DEATH

The *Mahabharata* guides those of Hindu faith to recognize that consumption of animal flesh undoubtedly involves the act of killing. It tells that the guilt of complicity of those involved in this process, including those slaughtering, selling, and consuming animal flesh, is upon all.

> *Thus, there are three forms of killings: he who brings the flesh or sends for it, he who cuts off the limbs of an animal, and he who purchases, sells or cooks flesh and eats it—all of these are to be considered meat-eaters.*
>
> Mahabharata[136]

The *Laws of Manu* teach that animal flesh can never be obtained without inflicting injury upon another.

> *Meat can never be obtained without injury to living creatures, and injury to sentient beings is detrimental to (the attainment of) heavenly bliss: let him therefore shun the use of meat.*
>
> Laws of Manu[137]

The *Tirukkural* tells that

> *If one realizes that meat is nothing but from the wound of another creature, one refrains from eating it.*
>
> Tirukkural[138]

Jain sacred teachings advise that one who consumes the flesh of another being, even if that being is killed by a third party, morally performs the act of killing.

> *If a man kills living things, or slays by the hand of another, or consents to another slaying, his sin goes on increasing.*
>
> *Sutrakrtanga*[139]

As expressed through the words of by Mahatma Gandhi,

> *In order to get meat, we have to kill.*
>
> Mahatma Gandhi[140]

The Philosophy of Vegetarianism

Through the cascade of steppingstones of philosophical thought created by the sacred scriptures of Hindu, Buddhist and Jain faiths, those of Indian heritage have been guided to live by sharing peace, compassion, and nonviolence with all beings. The sacred scriptures of each of these faiths, in and of themselves, hold enough wisdom to lead the populace of an entire nation to lives of nonviolence and vegetarianism.

Men of clear vision abstain from the flesh of a slaughtered animal.
Tirukkural[141]

The heart of a flesh-eater is devoid of love like that of the wielder of a deadly weapon.
Tirukkural[142]

He who injures innocent beings from a wish to give himself pleasure, never finds happiness, neither living nor dead.
Laws of Manu[143]

Grace is not killing, to kill disgrace: and to eat a thing killed, profitless sin.
Tirukkural[144]

Here in this long journey of birth-and-death there is no living being who . . . has not at some time been your mother or father, brother or sister, son or daughter . . . . So how can the bodhisattva [holy one] . . . eat the flesh of any living being.

Buddhism's *Lankavatara Sutra*[145]

Through his teachings of compassion, Emperor Asoka led the entire nation of India to adopt the virtues of nonviolence and vegetarianism.

Here no animal is to be killed for sacrifice . . . . Formerly in the Beloved of the God's kitchen several hundred thousand animals were killed daily for food; but now at the time of writing only three are killed . . . . Even these animals will not be killed in the future.

Inscription of Rock Edict I[146]

The sacred wisdom of vegetarianism of Hindu, Buddhist, and Jain faiths can be summed up by the words of Mahatma Gandhi

Spiritual progress does demand at some stage that we should cease to kill our fellow creatures for the satisfaction of our bodily wants.

Mahatma Gandhi[147]

PART III
CONCLUSION

WISDOM OF HINDU, BUDDHIST AND JAIN SACRED TEACHINGS
AND THE VEGETARIAN PHILOSOPHY OF INDIA

WISDOM OF HINDU, BUDDHIST AND JAIN SACRED TEACHINGS AND THE VEGETARIAN PHILOSOPHY OF INDIA

By understanding India's three great vegetarian faiths, the Hindu, Buddhist and Jain faiths, one gains insight into the origin of the vegetarian values that have pervaded its lands. The vegetarian values of India are deeply rooted within the traditions of each of these faiths, and the teachings of each faiths have fostered the cause of nonviolence amongst all. It is from these teachings of nonviolence that the deeply spiritual and profoundly philosophical beliefs in vegetarianism held by the people of India have emerged.

Because sacred teachings of each of these three vegetarian faiths are respected by individuals of each of the other two faiths, nonviolence has flourished within every corner of the Indian sub-continent. Many of these values attained widespread recognition during the era in which numerous disciples of Gautama Buddha, disciples of Mahavira, and sages of the Hindu faith were crisscrossing the Indian subcontinent, and sharing wisdom.[1]

Each of these belief systems contains spiritual and moral teachings of compassion and nonviolence. Each of these have served to reinforce the values of one another. In each of these traditions, holy individuals refrain from injuring or killing any living being. The primary vow of ascetics within each of these faiths is to live without harming and without killing.[2]

All three faiths have gifted the people of India with ethical, moral, and spiritual values greater than those attainable solely through the teachings of one faith. Their values have reinforced one another's values and have protected the lives of innumerable innocent creatures. They have also protected the souls of those human beings who practice them.

> *Do not get angry or harm any living creature, but be compassionate and gentle; show good will to all.*
> *Bhagavad Gita*[3]

The roots of the values of compassion, nonviolence and not harming upon the Indian sub-continent can be traced to the earliest sacred scriptures of the Hindu faith. They were cultivated and strengthened even further by sacred writings of the Buddhist and Jain faiths. Hence, one must appreciate and respect the teachings of each of India's three vegetarian faiths—Hindu, Buddhist and Jain faiths—for each has contributed to the advancement of nonviolence and vegetarianism throughout the entire nation of India.

The sum of the teachings of each of these three faiths have gifted the people of India with a strong foundation of ethical, moral, and spiritual values greater than would have been possible through the teachings of one faith alone.

May your knowledge of these teachings fill your life with wisdom, understanding, and compassion for all.

> *[In consuming the flesh of another being] we kill ourselves, our*
> *body and soul.*
>
> Mahatma Gandhi[4]

Part IV

Back Matter

INTRODUCTION

[1] Eknath Easwaran, *The Upanishads* (Tomales, CA: Nilgiri Press, 2000), 115.

[2] Mahatma Gandhi, *The Selected Works of Mahatma Gandhi*, vol V, *The Voice of Truth* (Ahmedabad, India: Navajivan Publishing, 1968), 234. (Extracted from *Young India*, 25-9-1924), 317-318.

PART I: BACKGROUND

[1] Basham, A.L. *The Wonder That was India*, 3rd revised edition (New Delhi: Rupa & Co., 2001. First published in 1954), 12.

[2] Abinas Chandra Das, *Ṛgvedic India: Cultural History of India as Depicted in the Ṛgveda*, vol I, Third Edition (New Delhi: Cosmo Publications, 1980), 7.

[3] Abinas Chandra Das, *Ṛgvedic India: Cultural History of India as Depicted in the Ṛgveda*, vol II, 581–585.

[4] Das, Abinas Chandra, vol I, 51.

[5] Ibid., vol I, 54.

[6] Ibid., vol I, 96.

[7] Bridget Allchin and Allchin, R. *The Birth of Indian Civilization* (Baltimore, MD: Penguin Press, 1968), 156–158.

[8] Ainslie T. Embree, ed., *Sources of Indian Tradition*, vol I (NY: Columbia University Press, 1988), 4.

[9] Das, Abinas Chandra, vol I, 12–17.

[10] Allchin, 296–307.

[11] Das, Abinas Chandra, vol I, 79.

[12] Basham, *Wonder That was India*, 18–23.

[13] Christopher Key Chapple, *Nonviolence to Animals, Earth, and Self in Asian Traditions* (Albany, NY: State University Press, 1993), 6–7.

[14] In Tamilnadu, which is a state in South India, people celebrate a festival called Pongal. The celebration lasts four days. On the third day, people decorate cattle, pay homage to them and pray to the essence of God within them.

[15] Allchin, 160.

[16] R.C. Majumdar, H.C. Raychaudhuri and Kalikinkar Datta, *An Advanced History of India* (London: Macmillan & Co., 1950), 19.

[17] Das, Abinas Chandra, vol I, xii–xiv.

[18] Chapple, 6-7.

[19] Tahtinen, Unto. *Ahimsa, Non-violence in Indian Tradition* (London: Rider & Co., 1976), 131–132.

[20] Allchin, 161–167.

[21] Ibid., 170–177.

[22] Basham, *Wonder That was India*, 28–29.

[23] Abinas Chandra Das, *ṚgVedic India* (vol I, 185-187), explains similarities between Greek and Slavic languages, and Sanskrit. He suggests that the former was derived in part from Sanskrit when people of the Sapta-Sindhu migrated to Iran, and then Europe. The Aryan languages (native to India) spread from India to west and north Europe through Semitic people who traveled during later ages between Indo-Irania and Europe (vol II), 353-371).

[24] Das, Abinas Chandra, vol. I, 148.

[25] Allchin and Allchin, *The Birth of Indian Civilization* (Baltimore, MD: Penguin Press, 1968), 176.

[26] S. Radhakrishnan, *The Hindu View of Life* (NY: MacMillian Co., 1971), 12.

[27] Ibid., 93.

[28] Ibid., 14.

[29] Rishis, through meditation, overcame desires and fears. They were able to communicate with God and informed the rest of humankind of what they learned through meditation.

[30] Swami Sivananda, *All About Hinduism* (Tehri-Garhwal, U.P., Himalayas, India: Divine Life Society, 1997), 14.

[31] Ibid., 14-15.

[32] Easwaran, *Upanishads*, 10–11.

[33] Das, Abinas Chandra, vol I, 7.

34 Easwaran, *Upanishads*, 10–11.

35 Lucille Schulberg, *Historic India* (NY: Time-Life Books, 1968), 36.

36 Troy Wilson Organ. *Hinduism: Its Historical Development* (NY: Barron's Educational Series, 1974), 93.

37 Basham, *Wonder That was India*, 42.

38 Rabbi Aryeh Kaplan, *The Living Torah* (Brooklyn, NY: Maznaim Publishing, 1981), 289. Animal sacrifice was not uncommon in ancient times. Leviticus 1.5 "When one of you brings a mammal as an offering to God, the sacrifice must be taken from the cattle, sheep or goat."

39 K.A. Nilakanta Sastri, *A History of South India*, Third edition (London: Oxford University Press, 1966), 63.

40 Basham, *Wonder That was India*, 35.

41 Swami Nikhilananda, *The Upanishads*, Vol I (NY: Ramakrishna-Vivekananda Center, 1990), 2–4.

42 Ibid., 3.

43 Sivananda, *All About Hinduism,* 17.

44 Brian K. Smith, "Eaters, Food, and Social Hierarchy in Ancient India," *Journal of the American Academy of Religion*, Summer, l vol LVIII, Number Two (1990): 177–181.

45 Swami Prabhavananda, *Vedic Religion and Philosophy* (Madras, India: Sri Ramakrishna Math, not dated), 37–39.

46 Ibid., 40.

47 Max F. Muller, ed. *The Sacred Books of the East.* vol XLII *Hymns of the Atharva Veda* (New Delhi: Motilal Banarsidass, 2000. First Published 1897), 214.

48 Nikhilananda, *Upanishads*, vol I, 11.

49 Radhakrishnan, *Hindu View of Life*, 24.

50 William Stoddart, *Outline of Hinduism* (Wash, DC: Foundation of Traditional Studies, 1993), 49.

51 Board of Scholars, trans. *The Siva-Purana* (New Delhi: Motilal Banarsidas, 1977), xi.

52 Stoddart, 59–63.

53 Prabhavananda, 103.

54 Eknath Easwaran, *The Bhagavad Gita* (Tomales, CA: Niligri Press, 2001), 5. Many believe that the *Bhagavad Gita* was written later than most of the *Mahabharata,* by an inspired seer such as Vyasa.

55 Sarvepalli Radhakrishnan and Charles A. Moore, ed. *A Sourcebook of Indian Philosophy* (Princeton, NJ: Princeton University Press, 1957), 164-173.

56 Ibid., ed. 164.

57 Ibid., ed. 164.

58 Kamala Subramaniam, *Mahabharata* (Mumbai, India: Bharatiya Vidya Bhavan, 2001), 153.

59 Basham, *A Cultural History of India* (New Delhi: Oxford University Press, 1975), 28–29.

60 Kamala Subramanian, *Ramayana*, 7th edition (Mumbai, India: Bharatiya Vidya Bhavan, 1998), v-vi.

61 Prabhavananda, 104.

62 Ibid., 125.

63 Richard D. Waterstone, *India* (London: Harper-Collins Publishers, 2002), 86.

64 Radhakrishnan and Moore, ed., 453.

65 Swami Venkatesananda, *The Yoga Sutras of Patanjali* (Tehri-Garhwal, India: Divine Life Society, 2001), 151–369.

66 Sandra Anderson and Rolf Sovik, *Yoga: Mastering the Basics* (Honesdale, PA: Himalayan Institute Press, 2000), 3.

67 Swami Muktibodhananda, *Hatha Yoga Pradipika* (Munger, Bihar, India: Yoga Publications Trust, 1993), 17–148.

68 Swami Vishnudevananda, *The Complete Illustrated Book of Yoga* (Simon & Schuster, NY, 1960), 1–208.

69 Surendranath Dasgupta, *Yoga as Philosophy and Religion* (New Delhi: Motilal Banarsidas, 1987. First Edition, London, 1924), 142.

70 Ibid., 141.

71 Radhakrishnan and Moore, ed., 467.

72 Venkatesananda, 216.

73 Dasgupta, 138.

74 Ibid., 139–140.

75 Patrick Olivelle, ed., *Dharmasutras, the Law Codes of Apastamba, Gautama, Baudhayana, and Vasistha* (NY: Oxford University Press, 1999), xxi.

76 Embree, 214.

77 Max F. Muller, ed. *The Sacred Books of the East.* vol XXV *The Laws of Manu* (New Delhi: Motilal

Banarsidass. 1996. First Published 1886), 1–30.

78 Tahtinen, 53.

79 Ramachandra V.R. Dikshitar *Tirukkural of Tiruvalluvar*, Second Edition (Madras, India: Adyar Library and Research centre, 1994), 67.

80 Hemant V.P. Kanitkar and W. Owen Cole, *Hinduism* (Abington, Oxon, England: Bookpoint, 1995), 141.

81 Radhakrishnan, *Hindu View of Life*, 18.

82 Radhakrishnan and Moore, ed., 506.

83 Kanitkar, 147.

84 Satischandra Chatterjee and Dhirendramohan Datta, *An Introduction to Indian Philosophy* 6th edition (Calcutta, India: University of Calcutta, 1960), 349.

85 Chatterjee and Datta, 365–366.

86 Ibid., 370-371.

87 Radakrishnan and Moore, ed., 511.

88 Chatterjee and Datta, 352.

89 Ibid., 353 (*Rig Veda*, 10.90 Peterson's translation).

90 Thus, when Hindus greet one another, one brings one's palms together, bowing to the essence of God within the other individual.

91 T.M.P. Mahadevan, *Outlines of Hinduism* (Bombay, India: Chetana Limited, 1956), 22–25.

92 Mohandas K. Gandhi, *The Bhagavad Gita According to Mahatma Gandhi* (Berkley, CA: Berkley Hills Books, 2000), 17.

93 Radhakrishnan and Moore, ed., 526.

94 Paul Deussen, trans., *Sixty Upanisads of the Veda*, Vol I and II (Motilal Banarsidass Publishers, 1997. First German Edition 1897), 611.

95 Easwaran, *Upanishads*, 109–110.

96 Easwaran, *Bhagavad Gita*, 116.

97 Swami Nikhilananda, *The Upanishads*, Vol II (NY: Ramakrishna-Vivekananda Center, 1990), 97.

98 Easwaran, *Bhagavad Gita*, 85.

99 Only human beings have the ability to fully eliminate negative *karma*, because of their ability to think and act purely. It is said that a soul has lived over a million lives before reaching a human stage.

100 To illustrate this concept, if one exhibits unusual aggression, one will be reborn in a lower life realm to exhaust these tendencies because lower forms of life do not have *karma*. Such an individual is thereby relieved from the need to be reborn in human form many times to work off this *karma*.

101 Stanley Rice, *Hindu Customs and their Origins* (New Delhi: Low Price Publications, 1937. Reproduced 1993), 195.

102 Rice, 196.

103 http://www.cmp.caltech.edu/chaos/ Lorenz. 11/12/2003.

104 Easwaran, *Upanishads*, 230.

105 Sivananda, *All About Hinduism*, 75–82.

106 Ibid., 66.

107 Sivananda, *Essence of Principal Upanishads* (Tehri-Garhwal, U.P., Himilayas, India: Divine Life Society, 1997), 7–8.

108 Easwaran, *Upanishads*, 229.

109 Das, Abinas Chandra, vol. I, 155.

110 Muller, *Sacred Books of the East*. XXV, *The Laws of Manu*, 175.

111 Nikhilananda, *Upanishads*, vol I, 122.

112 Basham, *Wonder That was India,* 42.

113 Waterstone, 18.

114 Wm. Theodore De Bary, ed. *Sources of Indian Tradition,* vol I (NY: Columbia University Press, 1985), 19-25.

115 Muller, *Sacred Books*, vol XXV, *Laws of Manu*, 173.

116 G.N. Das, *Readings from the Bhagavata* (New Delhi: Abhinac Publications, 1996), 65–66.

117 Tahtinen, 11.

118 G.N. Das, 67.

119 Easwaran, *Bhagavad Gita*, 66.

120 Tahtinen, 87.

121 G.N. Das, 100–101.

122 Rice, 135.

123 Ibid., 140-141.

124 Majumbar, Raychaudhuri, and Datta, 84.

125 Francis Zimmerman, *The Jungle and the Aroma of Meats: An Ecological Theme in Hindu Medicine* (Berkley, CA: University of California Press, 1987), 1–2.

126 Muller, *Sacred Books,* vol XXV, *Laws of Manu,* 177.

[127] Tahtinen, 35.

[128] Ibid., 53.

[129] Ibid., 109.

[130] P.S. Sundaram, *Tiruvalluvar, The Kural* (New Delhi: Penguin Books, 1990), 44.

[131] S. Radhakrishnan, *The Principal Upanishads* (New Delhi: Harper Collins India, 1994), 676.

[132] De Bary, 26.

[133] Radhakrishnan, *Principal Upanishads*, 677.

[134] Lionel D. Barnett. *Antiquities of India* (NY: G.P. Putnam's Sons, 1914), 158–159.

[135] Basham, *Wonder That was India*, 195.

[136] Ibid, 213.

[137] Sivananda, *All about Hinduism*, 72.

[138] Dikshitar, 67.

[139] Sivananda, *All about Hinduism,* 72.

[140] S. M. Batra, *Cows and Cow-slaughter in India: religious, political and social aspects* (The Hague, The Netherlands: Institute of Social Studies, ISS Occasional Papers, 1981), 2–3.

[141] Basham, *Wonder that was India*, 120.

[142] Beatrice Pitney Lamb, *India, a World in Transition, Third Edition* (NY: Praeger Publishers, 1968), 111.

[143] Lamb, 111.

[144] Mahatma Gandhi, *Hindu Dharma* (Ahmedabad, India: Navajivan Publishing, 1950), 297.

[145] Mahadevan, 79–82.

[146] F. Max Muller, ed. *Sacred Books of the East,* vol X, Part I and II *The Dhammapada* (New Delhi: Motilal Banarasidass, 1973. First published Oxford University Press, 1881), 67.

[147] Edward Conze, *A Short History of Buddhism* (London: George Allen & Unwin, 1980), 99–100.

[148] Organ, 145–146.

[149] Conze, 108–109.

[150] Tahtinen, 132. op cit : E. Thomas, *The History of Buddhist Thought* (London, Routledge,1951), 11.

[151] Tahtinen, 133,

[152] Embree, 192–193.

[153] Conze, 1.

[154] E. A. Burtt, ed. *The Teachings of the Compassionate Buddha* (NY: Penguin Putnam: 1955), 22–23.

[155] Ninian Smart, ed. *Atlas of World Religions*, NY: Oxford University Press, 1999), 24–25.

[156] Muller, *Sacred Books,* vol X, Part I, *Dhammapada*, liii.

[157] Ibid, 37.

[158] Narada Thera, *The Dhammapada, Pali Text and Translation* (Kuala Lumpur, Malaysia: Buddhist Missionary Society, 1978), viii.

[159] Eknath Easwaran, *The Dhammapada* (Tomales, CA: Nilgiri Press, 1985), 111.

[160] Muller, *Sacred Books,* vol X, *Dhammapada*, Part I, 36.

[161] Muller, *Sacred Books*, vol. X, *Dhammapada*, Part II, 25.

[162] Basham, *Wonder That was India*, 282.

[163] Muller, *Sacred Books,* vol X, *Dhammapada*, Part II, xi-xv.

[164] Ibid, 114.

[165] Ibid, 49.

[166] De Bary, 169–170.

[167] N. A. Nikam and Richard McKeon, ed and trans. *Edicts of Asoka* (Chicago: University of Chicago, 1959), 27

[168] Ibid, 28.

[169] Barnett, 46.

[170] Organ, 130.

[171] Nikam and McKeon, 1.

[172] Ibid., 30.

[173] Ibid, 30

[174] Ibid, 41.

[175] Basham, *Wonder that was India,* 54.

[176] Nikam and McKeon, 55.

[177] Basham, *Cultural History of India*, 46–48.

[178] Ibid, 52.

[179] Majumbar, Raychaudhuri and Datta, 159.

[180] Basham, *Wonder That was India*, 52.

[181] R.C. Dwivedi, *Contribution of Jainism to Indian Culture* (New Delhi: Motilal Banarsidass, 1975), 120.

[182] Tahtinen, 132.

[183] Paul Dundas, *The Jains*, Second Edition (London: Routledge, 2002), 19–24.

[184] Dwivedi, 121.

[185] F. Max Muller, *Sacred Books of the East, Jaina*

Sutras, vol XLV, Part II (New Delhi: Motilal Banarsidass, 1964. First published by Oxford University Press, 1895), 307.

[186] Padmanabh S. Jaini, *The Jaina Path of Purification* (New Delhi: Motilal Banarsidass, 1979), 169.

[187] Ibid, 47–48.

[188] Dundas, 177.

[189] De Bary, 57.

[190] Dundas, 97.

[191] Chapple,13.

[192] Ibid, 11–12.

[193] F. Max Muller, *Sacred Books of the East,* vol XXII, Part I *Jaina Sutras* (New Delhi: Motilal Banarsidass, 1964. First published Oxford University Press, 1884), 50.

[194] Jaini, 49–53.

[195] Ibid, 66.

[196] Embree, 67.

[197] Jaini, 138–150.

[198] Muller, *Sacred Books,* vol XLV, Part II, *Jaina Sutras,* 247.

[199] Jaini, 167.

[200] Muller, *Sacred Books,* vol XLV, Part II, *Jaina Sutras,* 286.

[201] Chapple, 3–4. Extracted from *Acaranga Sutra* translated by Nathmal Tatia, *Studies in Jaina Philosophy* (Banaras: Jain Cultural Research Society, 1951), 18.

[202] Muller, *Sacred Books,* vol XXII, Part I, *Jaina Sutras,* 1–11.

[203] Jaini, 173–174.

[204] Ibid, 167–168.

[205] Muller, *Sacred Books,* vol XXII, Part I, *Jaina Sutras,* 202.

[206] Dundas, 158.

[207] Muller, *Sacred Books,,* vol XXII, Part I, *Jaina Sutras,* 136.

[208] Organ, 135–140.

[209] M.K. Gandhi, *Diet and Reform* (Ahmedabad, India: Navajivan Publishing,1949), 3.

[210] Smart, 53.

[211] Ibid., 38.

PART II: THE SACRED TEACHINGS

[1] Nikhilananda, *Upanishads,*vol. I, 32.

[2] Prabhavananda, 45.

[3] Ibid, 47.

[4] Sivinanda, *Principal Upanishads, 18.*

[5] Ibid., 18.

[6] Nikhilananda, *Upanishads,*vol I, 39.

[7] Easwaran, *Upanishads,* 143.

[8] Sivananda, *Principal Upanishads,* 3–5.

[9] Subramaniam, *Mahabharata,* 492.

[10] Easwaran, *Upanishads,* 225.

[11] Radhakrishnan, *Principal Upanisads,* 234.

[12] Easwaran, *Bhagavad Gita,* 134.

[13] Radhakrishnan, *Hindu View of Life,* 24.

[14] Easwaran, *Upanishads,* 183.

[15] Nikhilananda, *Upanishads,* vol II, 132.

[16] Nikhilananda, *Upanishads,* vol I, 41.

[17] Radhakrishnan, *Principal Upanisads,* 34.

[18] Easwaran, *Upanishads,* 27-28.

[19] Radhakrishnan, *Principal Upanisads,* 553.

[20] Easwaran, *Upanishads,* 111–112.

[21] Sivananda, *Principal Upanishads,* 181.

[22] Easwaran, *Upanishads,* 130.

[23] Easwaran, *Bhagavad Gita,* 85.

[24] Easwaran, *Upanishads,* 208.

[25] Sivananda, *Principal Upanishads,* 181.

[26] Easwaran, *Upanishads,* 228.

[27] Ibid., 87.

[28] Radhakrishnan, *Hindu View of Life,* 19.

[29] Kanitkar, 101.

[30] Easwaran, *Upanishads,* 110.

[31] Radhakrishnan and Moore, ed., 51.

[32] Easwaran, *Upanishads,* 28.

[33] Chatterjee and Datta, 356.

[34] Radhakrishnan, *Principal Upanisads,* 876–877.

[35] Sivananda, *Principal Upanishads,* 32.

[36] Prabhavananda, 48.

[37] Nikhilananda, *Upanishads,* vol, I. 43–44.

[38] Easwaran, *Upanishads,* 24–25.

[39] Sivananda, *Principal Upanishads,* 3–5.

[40] Gandhi, *Selected Works,* vol. V, *Voice of Truth,* 86.

[41] Easwaran, *Upanishads,* 93.

42 Easwaran, *Upanishads*, 112.

43 Deussen, vol II, 548.

44 Das G. N., 93.

45 Deussen, vol II, 577.

46 Paul Deussen, trans. *Sixty Upanisads of the Vedas.* vol I (Delhi: Motilal Banarsidass, 1997), 314.

47 Sivananda, *Principal Upanishads, 47.*

48 Chatterjee and Datta, 370–371.

49 Radakrishnan and Moore, ed., 511.

50 Sivananda, *Hinduism*, 75–82.

51 Ibid., 66.

52 Easwaran, *Upanishads*, 224.

53 Ibid., 190.

54 Sivananda, *Principal Upanishads*, 3–5.

55 Ibid., 3-5.

56 Organ, 167.

57 Deussen, vol II, 548.

58 Organ, 167.

59 Ibid., 162.

60 Easwaran, *Bhagavad Gita*, 157.

61 Embree, 321.

62 Basham, *Wonder that was India*, 339.

63 Chatterjee and Datta, 397.

64 Easwaran, *Upanishads*, 36.

65 Dikshitar, 65.

66 Barnett, 172.

67 Easwaran, *Upanishads*, 48.

68 Dasgupta, 141.

69 I.K. Tamini, *The Science of Yoga* (Wheaton, Ill.: Philosophical Publishing House, 1972), 232.

70 Dikshitar, 65.

71 Muller, *Sacred Books,* vol X, *The Dhammapada* Part I, 36–37.

72 Deussen, vol. I, 169.

73 Easwaran, *Upanishads*, 218.

74 Muller, *Sacred Books*, vol XXV, *Laws of Manu*, 175.

75 Easwaran, *Upanishads,* 229.

76 Muller, *Sacred Books,* vol X, *Dhammapada,* Part I, 37.

77 Jaini, 107–111.

78 De Bary, 57.

79 Muller, *Sacred Books*, vol XLV, *Jaina Sutras,* Part II, 286.

80 Sivananda, *Principal Upanishads, 88.*

81 Easwaran, *Upanishads*, 167.

82 Redhakrishnan and Moore, ed., 69.

83 Subramaniam, *Mahabharata,* 842.

84 Deussen, vol. II, 586.

85 Mahadevan, 22–25.

86 Easwaran, *Bhagavad Gita*, 107.

87 Easwaran, *Upanishads*, 46.

88 Deussen, vol. I, 308.

89 Easwaran, *Upanishads*, 49.

90 Ibid., 70–72.

91 Ibid., 218.

92 Easwaran, *Bhagavad Gita*, 172.

93 Easwaran, *Upanishads*, 209.

94 Ibid., 144.

95 F. Max Muller, ed. *Sacred Books of the East,* Volume XV. *The Upanishads,* Part II (New Delhi: Motilal Banarsidass, 1997. First published Oxford University Press, 1884), 97.

96 Deussen, vol. II, 548.

97 Yogi Ramacharaka, *The Spirit of the Upanishads* (Chicago: Yogi Publication Society, 1907), 69–70.

98 Easwaran, *Upanishads*, 85.

99 Easwaran, *Bhagavad Gita*, 67.

100 Ibid., 135.

101 Gandhi, *Bhagavad Gita*, 108.

102 Easwaran, *Bhagavad Gita*, 107.

103 Ibid., 210.

104 Sri Jaidayal Dalmia, *A Review of 'Beef in Ancient India'* (New Delhi: Radha Press, 1971), 154.

105 Radhakrishnan and Moore, ed., 164.

106 Mahadevan, 229.

107 Ramacharaka, 54.

108 Easwaran, *Bhagavad Gita*, 190.

109 Nikhilananda, *Upanishads*, vol I, 206.

110 Ibid., 54.

111 Dalmia, 151.

112 Dalmia, 152.

113 Dikshitar, 65.

114 Muller, *Sacred Books,* vol XXV, *Laws of Manu,* 176.

115 Dikshitar, 67.

116 Radhakrishnan and Moore, ed., 165.

[117] Muller, *Sacred Books,* vol XXV. *Laws of Manu,* 176.

[118] Radhakrishnan and Moore, ed., 164.

[119] Venkatesananda, 216.

[120] Subramaniam, *Mahabharata,* 844.

[121] Radhakrishnan, *Principal Upanisads*, 172.

[122] Dasgupta, 138.

[123] Ibid., 139–140.

[124] Dundas, 158.

[125] Dalmia, 39.

[126] B. Kuppuswamy, *Dharma and Society, a Study in Social Values* (Delhi: Macmillan Company of India, 1977), 150.

[127] R. N. Lakhotia, *All You Wanted to Know about Vegetarianism* (New Delhi: Sterling Publishers, 2002), 74.

[128] Dikshitar, 53.

[129] Dalmia, 39.

[130] Muller, *Sacred Books,* vol X, *Dhammapada,* Part II, 50.

[131] G.N. Das, 100.

[132] Muller, *Sacred Books,* vol X, *Dhammapada,* Part II, 64.

[133] Nikam and McKeon, 40.

[134] Muller, *Sacred Books,* vol XLV, *Jaina Sutras,* Part II, 236.

[135] Ibid., 311.

[136] Lakhotia, 74.

[137] Muller, *Sacred Books,* vol XXV, *Laws of Manu,* 176.

[138] Dikshitar, 53.

[139] De Bary 49–51.

[140] M.K. Gandhi, *Key to Health* (Ahmedabad, India: Navajivan Publishing,1948, reprinted 1999), 8.

[141] Dikshitar, 53.

[142] Ibid., 53.

[143] Muller, *Sacred Books,* vol XXV, *Laws of Manu,* 176.

[144] Sundaram, 44.

[145] Embree, 170.

[146] Ibid., 144.

[147] M.K. Gandhi, *India's Case for Swaraj* (Bombay, India: Yeshanand Publishing, 1932), 402–403.

PART III: CONCLUSION

[1] Rice, 150–151.

[2] Muller, *Sacred Books,* vol XXII, *Jaina Sutras*, Part I, xxii-xxiii.

[3] Easwaran, *Bhagavad Gita*, 190.

[4] M.K. Gandhi, *The Moral Basis of Vegetarianism* (Ahmedabad, India: Navajian Publishing House, 1959), 22.

Ahimsa: Nonviolence in thought, word and deed.

Aparigraha: Abstention from taking gifts; noncovetousness; not harboring greed.

Aranyakas: Those portions of the *Vedas* that contain interpretations of the sacrifices.

Artha: Purpose, wish, desire.

Arthasastra: Buddhist teachings of the Four Noble Truths.

Aryans: The ancient people native to Northwest India who contributed to the formation of the *Vedas*.

Asoka (Ashoka): Emperor of all India during the third century BCE. He converted to Buddhism and spread vegetarian values throughout the entire country.

Asteya: Abstinence from theft.

Atman: The essence of *Brahman* (God) in the soul of each and every being.

Atmansiddhi: The goal of all human endeavors. It is one's personal search for inner moral and spiritual truth.

Basavesvara: A south Indian sage (1131-1167) who founded a movement of social reform concerning the caste system and the practice of animal sacrifice.

Brachmacharya: Control of one's desires to satisfy the cravings of one's sensory organs. The practice of celibacy.

Brahma: The Hindu Lord of creation. One of the dieties of the Hindu trinity.

Brahman: God. The essence from which all beings are born, live, and to which they return after death. *Brahman* is transcendent and formless. *Brahman* is the refuge of all, the supreme goal, the life principle, truth, and the inner Self of all beings.

Brahmanas: Those portions of the *Vedas* containing commentaries that, among other things, outline correct performance of ancient animal sacrifices.

Brahmins: Individuals of the priestly, and highest, caste of Hinduism's four castes.

Buddha (Gautama Siddhartha): Born in 563 BCE in Southern Nepal, the son of a chieftan. Founder of the Buddhist faith. Some Hindus perceive Buddha as the ninth incarnation of the Hindu god *Vishnu*, that form of God That protects.

Buddhism: The philosophy of morality, *karma*, and cyclic rebirth formulated by Gautama Buddha during the sixth to fifth century BCE.

Caste System: An ancient Indian system from Vedic times classifying society into four main groups: *brahmin, kshatriya, vaishya*, and *shudra*.

Dhammapada: The most well-known of Buddha's teachings of the "path" or the "way." It contains a collection of Buddha's teachings arranged into themes.

Dharma: The religiously ordained duty of a Hindu based on his or her age, education, occupation, and social position. One's duty to others and to God.

Dharma Sutras (*Dharma Shastras*): A compendium of ancient Indian laws and wisdom literature that helped form the foundation for Hindu values. It includes the *Laws of Manu*.

Ford-maker: Term applied to the Spiritual guides of the Jain faith that appear at specific times over the centuries. Also referred to as a *Tirthankara*.

Gandhi (Mahatma): Mohandas K. Gandhi, 1869-1948. The man who led India to independence in 1947 through nonviolent means. Gandhi was a man of strong Hindu faith and an ardent believer in nonviolence and vegetarianism.

Gupta Empire: A family empire that controlled India during the fourth century CE. The Guptas were great benefactors of both Buddhist and Hindu faiths.

Harijan: The category of individuals belonging to the fourth level of India's caste system, the *Shudras*. These individuals are also referred to as untouchables, or, as stated by Mahatma Gandhi, the children of God.

Harsha: A Hindu king who regained control of India from foreign invaders during the seventh century CE. He restored values of nonviolence and vegetarianism.

Himsa: Any act of violence including violent thoughts, words, and actions.

Indus Valley Civilization: The ancient Indian civilization of the Indus River Valley. Founders of the Harappa and Mohenjo Daro cultures.

Jain Faith: One of India's most ancient traditions. It is a nontheistic faith that places great emphasis upon concepts of *karma*, rebirth and nonviolence.

Jiva: External layers, or sheaths, placed around all beings and all in existence. They create superficial appearances of differences. The principle of life, the vital breath.

Kama: Love. A sacred virtue. Love for all.

Karma: A foundational Hindu belief that one's actions in prior lives affect one's fate in one's present and future lives. The term *karma* refers both to one's actions and to the results of one's actions.

Laws of Manu: Rules of conduct written between the second to first century BCE and perceived as "remembered" sacred law.

Mahabharata: One of the two great Indian epics (the *Ramayana* being the other), tracing spiritual and karmic events amongst a group of family members. Its teachings have contributed to the formation of Hindu values.

Madhva: (1199-1278) Philosopher of *Vedantic* literature supporting view of "dualism," also termed *dvaita*.

Mahavira: Born 468 BCE. Most recent Ford Maker, or spiritual guide, of the Jain faith.

Moksha: Hindu belief in salvation, or one's final joining with the Universal Soul.

Puranas: A voluminous source of Hindu doctrine and mythology containing insight into those spiritual teachings that have guided Hindu thought for generations.

Ramanuja: (1050-1137) Philosopher of *Vedantic* literature supporting the view of differentiated nondualism.

Ramayana: One of India's two great epics (the *Mahabharata* being the other). It traces the fate of the soul (represented by *Sita*) and has contributed to the formation of present day Hindu thought.

Ṛg Veda: The most ancient of the *Vedas*. Often considered the Hindu Bible. Its *mantras* (hymns) reveal great truths of existence.

Rishis: The holy individuals whose utterances revealed the wisdom of the *Upanishads* to humankind.

Samhitas (*Mantra-Samhitas*): Portion of the *Vedas* containing hymns in praise of *Vedic* Gods.

Samsara: A foundational Hindu belief in transmigration of the soul from one being to another in a cyclic continuum of lives.

Satya: Truthfulness in thought, word and deed. Considered a virtue in Hinduism.

Shankara: (788-820) Philosopher of *Vedantic* Literature supporting the view of "non-dualism," or *advaita*.

Smriti: Term used for that portion of Hindu literature derived from prophets, saints, and sages. It includes the *Sutras, Shastras* (text books), *Puranas, Ramayana, Mahabharata,* and the *Bhagavad Gita*.

Sruti: That portion of Hindu sacred scripture that had been Divinely revealed, originating directly from God. It consists of all aspects of the *Vedas*—the *Samhitas, Brahmanas, Aranyakas*, and *Upanishads*.

Sutras: Threads of religious-philosophical thought woven together to form sacred teachings.

Tamilnadu: The southeastern region of the Indian subcontinent. The site of origin of the *Tirukkural*.

Tirthankara: Spiritual guides of the Jain tradition, Mahavira was the twenty-fourth such guide.

Tirukkural: A compendium of ethical and philosophical teachings written in South India sometime between the second century BCE and the eighth century CE.

Upanishads: The last portion of each of the four *Vedas*. These scriptures contain the essence of Hinduism's metaphysical principles.

Vedanta: Philosophical treatises based upon the collected wisdom of the Hindu Sacred texts including the *Upanishads, Brahma Sutras,* and the *Bhagavad Gita*.

Vedas: The most ancient of all Hindu texts. They are perceived as being revealed by God. The four *Vedas* are the *Ṛg Veda, Yajur Veda, Sama Veda, Artharva Veda*.

REFERENCES

Allchin, Bridget, and Raymond Allchin. *The Birth of Indian Civilization*. Baltimore, MD: Penguin Press, 1968.

Anderson, Sandra and Rolf Sovik, *Yoga: Mastering the Basics*. Honesdale, PA: Himalayan Institute Press, 2000.

Barnett, Lionel D. *Antiquities of India*. NY: G.P. Putnam's Sons, 1914.

Basham, A.L. ed. *A Cultural History of India*. New Delhi: Oxford University Press, 1975.

Basham, A.L. *The Wonder that was India*, 3rd Revised Edition. New Delhi: Rupa & Co., 2001. First published in 1954.

Batra, S.M. *Cows and Cow-slaughter in India: religious, political and social aspects*. The Hague, The Netherlands: Institute of Social Studies, ISS Occasional Papers, 1981.

Board of Scholars, trans. *The Siva-Purana*. New Delhi: Motilal Banarsidas, 1977.

Burtt, E.A., ed. *The Teachings of the Compassionate Buddha*. NY: Penguin Putnam, 1955.

Chapple, Christopher Key. *Nonviolence to Animals, Earth, and Self in Asian Traditions*. Albany, NY: State University of New York Press, 1993.

Chatterjee, Satischandra and Dhirendramohan Datta, *An Introduction to Indian Philosophy*, 6th Edition. Calcutta: University of Calcutta, 1960.

Conze, Edward. *A Short History of Buddhism*. London: George Allen & Unwin, 1980.

Dalmia, Sri Jaidayal. *A Review of 'Beef in Ancient India.'* New Delhi: Radha Press, 1971.

Das, Abinas Chandra. *Ṛgvedic India: Cultural History of India as Depicted in the Ṛgveda*. Vol. I & II, Third Edition. New Delhi: Cosmos Publishing, 1980.

Das, G.N. *Readings from the Bhagavata*. New Delhi: Abhinac Publications, 1996.

Dasgupta, Surendranath. *Yoga as Philosophy and Religion*. New Delhi: Motilal Banarsidass, 1987. First Printed in London, 1924.

Deussen, Paul. trans. *Sixty Upanisads of the Veda*. Two Volumes. New Delhi: Motilal Banarsidass Publishers, 1997. First German Edition 1897.

De Bary, Wm. Theodore, ed. *Sources of Indian Tradition*, Vol. I. NY: Columbia University Press, 1985.

Dikshitar, Ramachandra V.R. *Tirukkural of Tiruvalluvar*, Second Edition. Madras, India: Adyar Library and Research Centre, 1994.

Dundas, Paul. *The Jains*, Second Edition. London: Routledge, 2002.

Dwivedi, R.C. *Contribution of Jainism to Indian Culture*. New Delhi: Motilal Banarsidass, 1975.

Easwaran, Eknath. *The Dhammapada*. Tomales, CA: Nilgiri Press, 1985.

Easwaran, Eknath, *The Upanishads*. Tomales, CA: Nilgiri Press, 1987.

Easwaran, Eknath, *The Bhagavad Gita*. Tomales, CA: Nilgiri Press, 2001.

Embree, Ainslie T. *Sources of Indian Tradition*, Second Edition, Vol I. NY: Columbia University Press, 1988. First Edition 1958.

Gandhi, M.K. *India's Case for Swaraj*. Bombay: Yeshanand Publishing, 1932.

Gandhi, M.K. *Key to Health*. Ahmedabad, India: Navajivan Publishing, 1948, reprint 1999.

Gandhi, M.K. *Diet and Reform*. Ahmedabad, India: Navajivan Publishing, 1949.

Gandhi, M.K. *Hindu Dharma*. Ahmedabad, India: Navajivan Publishing, 1950.

Gandhi, M.K. *The Moral Basis of Vegetarianism*. Ahmedabad, India: Navajivan Publishing, 1959, reprint 1999.

Gandhi, M.K. *The Selected Works of Mahatma Gandhi*, Volume V, *The Voice of Truth*. Ahmedabad, India: Navajivan Publishing, 1968.

Gandhi, M. K. *The Bhagavad Gita According to Mahatma Gandhi*. Berkley, CA: Berkley Hills Books, 2000.

Jaini, Padmanabh S. *The Jaina Path of Purification*. New Delhi: Motilal Banarsidass Publishers, 1979.

Kanitkar, V.P. (Hemant) and W. Owen Cole, *Hinduism*. Abington, Oxon, England: Bookpoint, 1995.

Kaplan, Rabbi Aryeh, *The Living Torah*. Brooklyn, NY: Maznaim Publishing. 1981.

Kuppuswamy, B. *Dharma and Society, a Study in Social Values*. New Delhi: Macmillan Co. of India, 1977.

Lakhotia, R.N. *All You Wanted to Know about Vegetarianism*. New Delhi, Sterling Publishers, 2002.

Lamb, Beatrice Pitney. *India, a World in Transition*. Third Edition. NY: Praeger Publishers, 1968.

http://www.cmp.caltech.edu/chaos/ Lorenz. 11/12/2003.

Mahadevan, T.M.P. *Outlines of Hinduism.* Bombay, India: Chetana Limited, 1956.

Majumdar, R.C., H. C. Raychaudhuri, and Kalikinkar Datta. *An Advanced History of India.* London: Macmillan & Co., 1950.

Muktibodhananda, Swami, *Hatha Yoga Padipika.* Munger, Bihar, India: Yoga Publications Trust, 1993.

Muller, F. Max, ed. *The Sacred Books of the East, The Laws of Manu.* Vol XXV. New Delhi, Motilal Banarsidass, 1996. First published Oxford University Press, 1886.

Muller, F. Max, ed. *The Sacred Books of the East, The Dhammapada*, Vol X, Part I & II. New Delhi: Motilal Banarasidass, 1973. First published by Oxford University Press, 1881.

Muller, F. Max, ed. *The Sacred Books of the East, The Upanishads*, Vol XV. Part II. New Delhi: Motilal Banarsidass, 1997. First published Oxford University Press, 1884.

Muller, F. Max, ed. *The Sacred Books of the East, Jaina Sutras*, Vol XXII, part I. New Delhi: Motilal Banarsidass, 1964. First published Oxford University Press, 1884.

Muller, F. Max, ed. *The Sacred Books of the East. Hymns of the Atharva Veda,* Vol XLII. New Delhi:Motilal Banarsidass, 2000. First Published 1897).

Muller, F. Max, ed. *The Sacred Books of the East, Jaina Sutras*, Vol XLV, part II. New Delhi: Motilal Banarsidass, 1964. First published Oxford University Press, 1895.

Nikam, N.A. and Richard McKeon, ed. and trans. *The Edicts of Asoka.* Chicago, Ill: Chicago University Press, 1959.

Nikhilananda, Swami. *The Upanishads: A New Translation*, Vol I, Fifth Edition. NY: Ramakrishna-Vivekananda Center, 1990.

Nikhilananda, Swami. *The Upanishads: A New Translation*, Vol II, Third Edition. NY: Ramakrishna-Vivekananda Center, 1990.

Olivelle, Patrick, ed. *Dharmasutras, the Law Codes of Apastamba, Gautama, Baudhayana, and Vasistha.* NY: Oxford University Press, 1999.

Organ, Troy Wilson. *Hinduism: Its Historical Development.* NY: Barron's Educational Series, 1974.

Prabhavananda, Swami. *Vedic Religion and Philosophy.* Madras, India: Sri Ramakrishna Math, not dated.

Radhakrishnan, S. *The Hindu View of Life.* NY: MacMillan Company, 1971.

Radhakrishnan, S. *The Principal Upanishads.* New Delhi: Harper Collins India, 1994.

Radhakrishnan, Sarvepalli and Charles A. Moore, ed. *A Sourcebook of Indian Philosophy*. Princeton, NJ: Princeton University Press, 1957.

Ramacharaka, Yogi. *The Spirit of the Upanishads*. Chicago: Yogi Publication Society, 1907.

Rice, Stanley. *Hindu Customs and their Origins*. New Delhi: Low Price Publications, 1937. Reproduced 1993.

Sastri, K.A. Nilakanta. *A History of South India*, 3rd ed. London: Oxford University Press, 1966.

Schulberg, Lucille. *Historic India*. NY: Time-Life Books, 1968.

Sivananda, Swami. *All About Hinduism*. Tehri-Garhwal, U.P., Himalayas, India: Divine Life Society, 1997.

Sivananda, Swami. *The Essence of Principal Upanishads*. Tehri-Garhwal, Himalayas: Yoga–Vedanta Forest Academy, 1961.

Smart, Ninian, ed. *Atlas of World Religions*. NY: Oxford University Press, 1999.

Smith, Brian K. "Eaters, Food, and Social Hierarchy in Ancient India." *Journal of the American Academy of Religion*, Summer, Vol LVIII, Number Two (1990): 177–203.

Stoddart, William. *Outline of Hinduism*. Wash., D.C.: Foundation of Traditional Studies, 1993.

Subramaniam, Kamala. *Mahabharata*. Mumbai, India: Bharatiya Vidya Bhavan, 2001.

Subramanian, Kamala. *Ramayana*, 7th edition. Mumbai, India: Bharatiya Vidya Bhavan, 1998.

Sundaram, P.S. *Tiruvalluvar, The Kural*. New Delhi: Penguin Books, 1990.

Tahtinen, Unto. *Ahimsa, Non-violence in Indian Tradition*. London: Rider and Company, 1976.

Tamini, I.K., *The Science of Yoga*. Wheaton, Ill: Philosophical Publishing House, 1972.

Thera, Narada. *The Dhammapada, Pali Text and Translation*. Kuala Lumpur, Malaysia: Buddhist Missionary Society, 1978.

Venkatesananda, Swami. *Yoga Sutras of Patanjali*. Tehri-Garhwal, Himalayas, India: Divine Life Society, 2001.

Vishnudevananda, Swami, *The Complete Illustrated Book of Yoga*. NY: Simon & Schuster, 1960.

Waterstone, Richard D. *India*. London: Harper Collins Publishers, 2002.

Zimmerman, Francis. *The Jungle and the Aroma of Meats, An Ecological Theme in Hindu Medicine*. Berkley, CA: University of California Press, 1987.

INDEX OF QUOTATIONS

Part I Background: Quotation Number in Nonitaliced Numeral
Part II Sacred Teachings: Quotation Number in Italiced Numeral

HINDU TEACHINGS

BUDDHIST TEACHINGS

Printed in the United States
43003LVS00004B/5-104